PASTORAL PRESENCE
AND THE
DIOCESAN PRIEST

PASTORAL PRESENCE
AND THE
DIOCESAN PRIEST

PAUL T. KEYES

AFFIRMATION BOOKS
WHITINSVILLE, MASSACHUSETTS

Acknowledgments

Quotations from *The Edge of Sadness* by Edwin O'Connor, by permission of Little, Brown and Co. in association with the Atlantic Monthly Press. Copyright © 1961 by Edwin O'Connor

Library of Congress Cataloging in Publication Data

Keyes, Paul T., 1936–
    Pastoral presence and the diocesan priest.

    1. Pastoral theology—Catholic Church.
2. Clergy—Office. I. Title.
BX1913.K44   253   78-22009
ISBN 0-89571-004-8

Printed by Mercantile Printing Company, Worcester, MA
United States of America

To all the many good shepherds who have led me and others to a deeper openness and presence to the mystery of God's life and power in the ordinary rhythms of everyday life.

CONTENTS

FOREWORD

In this book, Father Paul Keyes shares a special gift of insight with all of the Christian community in general and with those of us who have been chosen to serve in the diocesan priesthood in particular. His gift is one of invitation; he invites us to live *reflectively,* not *reactively* like so many men in diocesan ministry.

As a diocesan priest involved in the pastoral care and counseling of other priests, I fully agree with Father Keyes's statement: "If the modern American parish priest is guilty of anything, it might be that he has often tried too hard." Such priests work so hard for the apostolate in the name of the Good Shepherd that if he were to walk into the room, they would be too busy doing "holy work" to even see or recognize him.

I am personally so happy to be a priest. I can think of nothing else I would rather be. Yet, like all priests in the Church today, the Church yesterday, and the Church tomorrow, I am consistently aware of the serious challenges before me to be a counter-culture person, i.e., an imitator of Christ. Father Raymond

Brown ends a biblical reflection on the priesthood by reminding us: "I mentioned that some of the 'identity crisis' among priests today may be related to different conceptions of priestly activity; but on a deeper level I would think that the only identity crisis truly worthy of the name occurs when, amidst the legitimate differences in priestly work, the priest begins to forget that it is Jesus Christ to whom he is bearing witness. Whatever other claim he may make about what he does, in order to know who he is, a priest must be able to join with Paul in issuing the challenge, 'Become imitators of me as I am of Christ' (1 Cor. 11:1)" (*Priest and Bishop: Biblical Reflections,* p. 44).

Father Keyes invites those of us who are diocesan priests to be imitators of Christ. In so doing, Father Keyes displays a particular sensitivity to our human and spiritual needs of growth and maturation. In certain ways, this book is reminiscent of Dom Chautard's *The Soul of the Apostolate.* It too argues that we must take care of ourselves physically, emotionally, intellectually, and spiritually if we are to be effective ministers of the Lord.

This book is not a canonical or historical exploration; nor is it a sociological or theological treatise. It is simply a spiritual book whose contents require reflection. In considering the message of this book, the reader would do well to keep in mind Father Donald Wuerl's keen insight in the introduction to his book, *The Catholic Priesthood Today*: "Vocation and priesthood are not merely patterns of human behavior; they are also operations of divine grace, and as such, they lie beyond our understanding" (pp. 10-11). Father Keyes invites the diocesan priest to ponder and to allow mystery in his own life and to trust in the graces that the Lord freely gives.

Seminarians preparing for parish ministry will find Father Keyes's meditation on John the Baptist compelling in its invitation to authenticity of Christian witness. It is evident that the author has learned not only from the experiences of his brother priests but also from his own experiences as a spiritual director and seminary professor.

This book is but one part of Father Keyes's graduate thesis entitled "Personal Care and Pastoral Presence," presented to the Institute of Man at Duquesne University. I thank Father Keyes for allowing Affirmation Books to publish this material in *Pastoral Presence and the Diocesan Priest*.

Reading this book will benefit priests, seminarians, and all persons concerned with diocesan ministry. I trust that upon reflecting on the contents of this book many priests will have renewed enthusiasm and sustained encouragement and will make the words of St. Leo the Great to the Christian community their own: "Dearly Beloved, it is not with bold presumption that we, mindful of divine goodness, honor the day on which we accepted the office of priesthood. For we confess in all gratitude and truth that, whatever good we may do in the exercise of our ministry, it is Christ Himself who works in us. Hence we rejoice not in ourselves, who can do nothing without Him, but in Him who gives us the possibility of acting for Him" (Sermon 5, 4; PL 54, 154).

Thomas A. Kane, Ph.D., D.P.S.
Priest, Diocese of Worcester
International Executive Director
House of Affirmation

Feast of St. John Chrysostom
September 13, 1978

A REFLECTION
ON MY PRIESTLY PRESENCE

All of us, gazing on the Lord's glory with unveiled faces, are being transformed from glory to glory into his very image by the Lord who is the Spirit. Because we possess this ministry through God's mercy, we do not give in to discouragement. It is not ourselves we preach but Christ Jesus as Lord, and ourselves as your servants for Jesus' sake. This treasure we possess in earthen vessels to make it clear that its surpassing power comes from God and not from us. We are afflicted in every way possible, but we are not crushed; full of doubts, we never despair. Continually we carry about in our bodies the dying of Jesus, so that in our bodies the life of Jesus may also be revealed. While we live we are constantly being delivered to death for Jesus' sake, so that the life of Jesus may be revealed in our mortal flesh.

(2 Cor. 3:18; 4-1, 5, 7-8, 10-11)

*Every high priest has been taken out of mankind and is
appointed to act for men in their relations with God, to
offer gifts and sacrifices for sins; and so he can sympathize with those who are ignorant or uncertain because
he too lives in the limitations of weakness.*

(Heb. 5:1)

*"I tell you most solemnly, anyone who does not enter
the sheepfold through the gate, but gets in some other
way is a thief and a brigand. The one who enters
through the gate is the shepherd of the flock; the gate-
keeper lets him in, the sheep hear his voice, one by one
he calls his own sheep and leads them out. When he has
brought out his flock, he goes ahead of them, and the
sheep follow because they know his voice. They never
follow a stranger but run away from him: they do not
recognize the voice of strangers."*

*Jesus told them this parable, but they failed to under-
stand what he meant by telling it to them.*

So Jesus spoke to them again:

"I tell you most solemnly,
I am the gate of the sheepfold.
All others who have come are thieves and
    brigands; but the sheep took no notice of them.
I am the gate.
Anyone who enters through me will be safe:
He will go freely in and out
and be sure of finding pasture.
The thief comes
only to steal and kill and destroy.
I have come
so that they may have life
and have it to the full.
I am the good shepherd:

the good shepherd is one who lays down his life
   for his sheep.
The hired man, since he is not the shepherd
and the sheep do not belong to him,
abandons the sheep and runs away
as soon as he sees a wolf coming,
and then the wolf attacks and scatters the sheep;
this is because he is only a hired man
and has no concern for the sheep.
I am the good shepherd;
I know my own
and my own know me
just as the Father knows me
and I know the Father;
and I lay down my life for my sheep.
And there are other sheep I have
that are not of this fold,
and these I have to lead as well.
They too will listen to my voice,
and there will be only one flock,
and one shepherd.
The Father loves me,
because I lay down my life
in order to take it up again.
No one takes it from me;
I lay it down of my own free will,
And as it is in my power to lay it down,
so it is in my power to take it up again;
and this is the command I have been given
   by my father. . . .
The sheep that belong to me listen to my voice;
I know them and they follow me.
I give them eternal life;
they will never be lost
and no one will ever steal them from me.

*The Father who gave them to me is greater than
    anyone,
and no one can steal from the Father.
The Father and I are one."*
                                (John 10:1-18, 27-30)[1]

I want to share an interesting experience. I spent ten years as a
parish priest before coming to the Center for the Study of Spirituality at the Institute of Man, Duquesne University in Pittsburgh. While I was studying I took up residence with the Passionist Fathers and Brothers at Saint Paul's Monastery. I had
been at the monastery for about two weeks when the following
incident happened to me. I stopped in the kitchen one morning
for a coffee break. One of the cooks, who is a lay woman, asked
me the question, "Father . . . you are new around here . . . what
Passionist house did you come from?" Smiling, I answered, "I
come from the Boston area." I was going to elaborate a little
when she suddenly interrupted and said, "Oh yes, I know many
of the Passionist priests from Boston." She then proceeded to
go through a litany of living saints whom she knew, not one of
whom I had ever heard of. She then said, "Father, you must
know Father X, and if you don't know him, you must have
known Father Y." Again I smiled and said, "I guess I must have
misled you. I am not a Passionist priest. I am a secular priest
from the diocese of Boston, and I am afraid I don't know the
Passionists in Boston." Immediately a startled look came across
her face and she said, "Oh . . . I'm sorry . . . you are just one of
those 'ordinary' priests like the priests in my parish." I laughed
good naturedly and replied, "Yes, I'm just one of those 'ordinary' priests." She then became a little bit embarrassed and
sputtered, "Oh, Father, please don't misunderstand . . . it's just
that . . . it's just that I thought you were one of the Passionists

1. *The Jerusalem Bible* (Garden City, NY: Doubleday and Co., 1971).
All scripture references in this chapter are taken from this source.

. . . I'm sorry . . . I hope I didn't hurt you by calling you an 'ordinary' priest.'' I laughed and answered, ''No, my friend, there is nothing to be sorry about. In fact you have paid me a great compliment by calling me just an 'ordinary' priest, for I hope that is what I am.''

I do not think I will ever forget this little conversation with my kitchen friend, for in just one sentence she summed up the whole meaning of what it means to be a secular parish priest. Of course, her definition of my priestly presence was quickly seized upon by my Passionist friends, and for three years I was kiddingly referred to as the "ordinary priest." In the humor, however, there grew in me a deeper reflection on what "just being an ordinary priest" really means. I began to think more and more about the great dignity there is in being a priest who lives intimately in the life and concerns of common, everyday people. I began to dwell on the mystery of what it means to be an ordinary person called to possess the magnificent Christ-like treasure of priesthood in the "earthen vessel" of a humanity that lives in the limitations of weakness.

The ordinary priest possesses this treasure of God's presence through God's mercy. The power of Christ's treasure does not come from me but from the surpassing power of God. As an ordinary priest, I can be afflicted in every way possible, but, I hope, not crushed. I can be full of doubts, but, I hope, not give in to despair. I can carry in my body the dying Jesus so that, I hope, the life of Jesus may be revealed. I have been taken out of mankind and appointed to act for men in their relations with God. I am a servant for Jesus' sake. I offer gifts and sacrifice for sins, and I can sympathize and care for those who are ignorant or uncertain because I too live in the limiting weakness of being just an ordinary person.

As my reflection continued, I noticed that there is a great deal written today about the priest as a radical witness of Christ's presence in the world. I went to my dictionary and discovered that the word "radical" comes from the Latin word *radix,* which means "root." A radical person is one who is "rooted or fundamentally original."[2] The radical witness of the secular parish priest rests in Christ's call to root his priestly presence in the rhythm of commonplace, everyday life. The parish priest is, in fact, the local extension of the Ordinary or Bishop of a diocese. The word "ordinary" comes from the Latin *ordinarius,* which means "order, or an officer who has immediate and original jurisdiction in his own right." Ordinary also is defined, "as pertaining to the common people, of common rank, quality or ability, not distinguished in any way but commonplace."[3] The Ordinary of a diocese is called to immediate and original spiritual jurisdiction over and care for the souls of his territory. The dictionary also offers an interesting insight into the word "diocese." The word comes from the Greek *dioikein,* which means "to keep house or to manage." *Oikos* means "house"; *dia* means "through"; and *oikein* means "to manage a household."[4] In each diocese, the Ordinary's care for his spiritual household is extended to the parish level. The word "parish" comes from the Greek word *paroikos,* which means "dwelling beside or near." *Para* means "beside" and again *oikos* means "house or dwelling."[5]

The radical presence or witness of the parish priest is to be the fundamental or original presence of God's care, God's "dwelling beside or near" the "ordinary and commonplace household" of his people. To be an ordinary priest carries the great dignity and responsibility of being called by Christ to live or dwell near ordinary people in their common, everyday, spiritual, and temporal needs. At the ordination ceremony every priest utters the words *Adsum* and *Promitto* to his Bishop.

---

2. *Webster's New International Dictionary* (Springfield, MA: G. & C. Merriam Co., 1955), p. 2,051.
3. Ibid., p. 1,717.
4. Ibid., p. 734.
5. Ibid., p. 1,777.

Translated, these words mean: "I am present. . . . I promise faithfully and obediently to accept the call of sharing in the ministry of the Ordinary of this diocese." The *Adsum* and the *Promitto* of the priest's ordination are continuing and moment-to-moment promises to be present to the spiritual and temporal care of the people entrusted to the priest's local dwelling place in the world, the parish.

In this book I will emphasize the important place personal presence has in the mystery of a genuine and authentic care. In a beautiful way, the parish priest is called to live as a deeply caring *dasein* with his people.[6] His existence is a standing out in the situatedness of common day-to-day life. He is called to dwell near his people (*para-oikein*), to be-there-with (*dasein*) his people. This dwelling near his people was dramatically and essentially proclaimed as the "good news" of Christ's mysterious presence when he called himself "the Good Shepherd." Originally, a pastor was a shepherd of goats or sheep. He cared for his flock by tending over them and feeding them. He lived in grazing areas far away from the metropolitan population of the cities. In fact, by the time of Jesus' coming into the history of man the shepherd was looked down upon by the general populace. Shepherds carried a reputation of being uncouth and vulgar. They were men who lived without the advantages of formal education, and they were unable to be faithful to the temple services and ritual of the Jewish Law. They were considered worldly and very common in a pejorative sense.

But Jesus said of himself: "I am the Good Shepherd; the Good Shepherd is one who lays down his life for his sheep. . . . the hired man, since he is not the shepherd and the sheep do not belong to him, abandons the sheep and runs away as soon as he

---

6. I am using the term *dasein* to mean the personal presence of "being-there." I discuss this term of Martin Heidegger on pp. 22-24 of my unpublished thesis *Personal Care and Pastoral Presence* (Ann Arbor, MI: University Microfilms, 1975).

sees a wolf coming, and then the wolf attacks and scatters the sheep; this is because he is only a hired man and has no concern for the sheep'' (John 10:11-13). Jesus transforms the whole presence of the common shepherd into the sign of His own concern and care for His people. The pastoral presence of the parish priest is the call to live this model of the Good Shepherd. In fact, the word "pastor" comes from the Latin word *pascere* and the Greek word *pateisthai,* which means "to feed or nurture."[7]

The pastor or the good shepherd cares for his people by living with and near them. He nurtures his people with New Bread and Living Water. As a diocesan parish priest, I am called to be the shepherd who leads his flock through the one gate who is Christ. I am called to proclaim not my own voice but his voice. If the people hear his voice living in me, I may not only lead them into deeper presence with the Lord but also encourage them by leading them out to the daily cares and concerns of everyday life. Yet, if they hear only my voice and not Christ's, they hear only the voice of a stranger. Not hearing his voice, they will run away and be separated because they do not recognize the voice of strangers. If Christ truly lives in me, then any person who enters through me will be safe. They will go in and out and be sure of finding pasture because the true ground, the true pasture of my life as a parish priest, is the presence of Christ.

The thief, the brigand, the hireling may emerge in me when I am no longer open to Christ's presence living in me. I may live by my own ideal self-image of what the priest should be for his people. I may live a life of constantly saying, "Yes, I know . . . I see . . . we'll do it this way." Doing it "this way" means usually doing it "my way." Often I am unwilling to lay down my ideal self and be real to the point of letting Christ come that they may have life and have it to the full. For the priest the wolf is not always "out there." Most of the time he is right "in here." The wolf is often me, my closed heart. This wolf living in me, this

---

7. *Webster's,* p. 1,789.

oftentimes pridefully inflated me, this ideal me who searches too regularly for his own self-glorification scatters the sheep. In Christ's terms I can become the hireling because I have no real concern for the sheep. My concern is often drained off in a counterfeit bootlegging of self.

But to lay down my life for the sheep is to find the courage to live as well as to say, "Yes, I don't know . . . I don't see . . . we'll do it His way." Only Christ, ultimately, knows his own, and his own know him. He knows them just as his Father knows him and he knows the Father. Christ always knows the flock with the eyes of his Father, and he asks me as priest to know them not as I think I know them but to know them as he and his Father know them, to know them as his children, his friends. In this caring to know my people as Christ knows them, I too must lay down my life, for I am constantly being delivered to death for Jesus' sake. I must learn to live the paschal mystery of everyday life, dying to my old self and rising to the caring presence of Christ living in me. I have the power to lay my life down in imitation of the good shepherd, but only Christ possesses the power to take my life up again. He alone possesses the power to transform me into a new creation, for this is the command given to him by his Father. Through the gift of the Spirit, he pneumatizes my caring "sarx."[8] I am lifted up in Christ.

In renewing my priesthood in the paschal mystery of Christ's model of death and resurrection, I can then, and only then, care with his care. I will be able to give my people eternal life, for as Saint Paul so magnificently said: "I can live for God. I have been crucified with Christ, and I live now not with my own life but with the life of Christ who lives in me" (Gal. 2:19-20). In listening to my voice, the parishioners who live nearby me *(para-*

---

8. The term "pneumatize" in Christian theology means the elevated glorification of reality by the Holy Spirit. "Sarx" means my human nature. Once Christ ascended to his Father, he sent the Holy Spirit into the world to transform man into a new creation. I discuss this meaning on pp. 369-71 of *Personal Care and Pastoral Presence.*

oikein) will truly belong to Christ and listen to his voice. In following me, they will follow him. They will not be lost and scattered, for no one will be able to steal them from him. The Father who entrusted these wonderful people to Christ living in me is greater than anyone. Christ assures us that no one can steal from his Father, for the Father and Christ are one. In my pastoral ministry, the Holy Trinity dwells nearby the *oikon,* the household of His people. In fact, the Church is God's people. As pastor, I nurture God's ordinary people with the extraordinary food of the sacraments. I break open the bread of the Living Word. Through my person, Christ heals their many wounds and calls forth their unique gifts. Yes, I have been taken out of mankind into Christ in order to act for men in their relations with God. Living nearby and with one another, we walk together in Christ the daily road to Emmaus.

OBSTACLES TO PASTORAL CARE

This treasure we possess in earthen vessels. . . . (2 Cor. 4:7)

In this chapter I want to explore the obstacles in a parish priest's life that make it difficult for him to be the good shepherd. The parish priest is not an extraordinary person but a very ordinary man living in the common rhythms of everyday life. As a secular priest, I am called to live among and minister to the souls entrusted to me in the parish milieu. At the Last Supper, Christ spoke to me when he sent his disciples into the world with the words:

> I am not asking you to remove them from the world, but to protect them from the evil one. They do not belong to the world any more than I belong to the world. Consecrate them in the truth; your word is truth. As you sent me into the world, I have sent them into the world, and for their sake I consecrate myself so that they too may be consecrated in truth.
>
> (John 17:15-19)

To live and care for souls in the world is my summons. Therefore, I want to discuss the day-to-day life of a parish priest and the various obstacles that may influence his life and interfere with his consecration in the Father's truth. My thoughts on this

23

subject will flow from scholarly considerations as well as from my own ten-year experience as an active parish priest.

TOTALIZING THE FUNCTIONAL MODEL OF MAN

As a human being, I am always existing or standing out in my world. Martin Heidegger describes my humanity with the German term *dasein,* which means that as a man I am always "being-there-with-my-world." I am always standing out in relation to my world by the very nature of my human existence (*exsistere* in Latin means to "stand out"). Adrian van Kaam's personality theory helps me understand that I am being-there in the world through the interacting participation of three levels of personality: my vital self, my personal self, and my spirit self. Because my existence is always the basic issue of my life, I am concerned fundamentally for and about this existence. This fundamental concern for my own existence marks my existential care in the everyday world. I care for my existence on each of my personal dimensions. I can care for good food that nourishes my body. I can care to work in order to make a living. I can care to open myself to the intimate presence of God through prayer.

Separation or personal alienation enters my life when I totalize the little cares of life as ultimate cares. I separate myself from the ultimate horizon of all life, which is the mystery of God. This tendency to totalize a "little beyond" for the "Big Beyond" happens to all men.[1] Therefore, it becomes important for all men to consider reflectively how this temptation to totalize isolates them from a deeper integration with the wholeness of life. As a parish priest, I can live in a world in which the voice of the anonymous "they," the voice of the crowd, encourages me to be the tireless worker. I can begin more and more to totalize the functional articulation of my personal dimension as "the" way to find my place.

---

1. Refer to *Personal Care and Pastoral Presence,* pp. 14-15, wherein I discuss Adrian van Kaam's personality theory and the tendency man has to totalize partial wholes.

In fixating myself in the model of the priest who is always working, I can live with my own functional expectations as well as with the functional expectations of the crowd. I begin to believe that to be a success demands complete absorption in working for the Lord. I am always on the job or on duty. I find it difficult to "waste time" on myself or get away for a day off, to say nothing of a relaxing vacation. The care of souls becomes translated into slavish work. My pastor is my "boss." Fellow priests in the parish are my fellow "workers." If I preach a fine sermon, people may say to me, "Good job, Father!" In such a functional modality, people quickly become problems and a never-ending stream of interruptions. The more work I prove I can do, the more work my "boss" will entrust to me. I learn quickly as a young priest that I can win approval and affirmation from my pastor, from fellow priests, and from parishioners by being highly efficient, well organized, and tireless. Even my parents will ask, "Well, what project are you working on now?" When I gather with priest friends, we constantly compare notes on what we are "doing." What we are doing always seems ever so much more important than who we are. We attempt to become specialists in certain fields very quickly. Some choose to be great counselors, ecumenists, or liturgists. Others choose to build youth organizations or work tirelessly in newly emerging opportunities in the social apostolate. There is a never-ending litany of projects and causes in which we can "lose" ourselves.

A TYPICAL DAY

I will share a typical day in my parish life to show that what I am suggesting is not out of the question. Of course, my experience is certainly not inclusive of all parish priests' lives, but I do think that it does indicate a profile of day-to-day life in the parish. Parish priests may recognize better than anyone else what I am portraying. I usually get up at 6:15 A.M. each morning. After putting myself together, I am unlocking the Church at 6:40 A.M.

Without too much prayerful preparation, I celebrate the seven o'clock Mass. At the conclusion of Mass, someone will undoubtedly walk into the sacristy and want some kind of information or assistance with some pressing problem or concern. By 8:00 A.M. I am back in the rectory without too much attention given to a prayerful thanksgiving after Mass. I gulp down some coffee and cereal and try to catch up on the latest news in the morning newspaper. As I am eating breakfast, the pastor, one of my fellow assistants, the janitor, or the telephone very often will pull me away from this relaxed pause to some concern over a problem or project that lies ahead of me that day.

At nine o'clock I may have two hours of communion calls at various houses in the parish; I may have to attend the monthly meeting of the area clergy; or I may have the nine o'clock funeral liturgy, burial services, and a visit to the home of the bereaved. I may have to see a woman who called last night and was distressed about a family problem; I may visit the parochial school to teach a class on religion; or I may stop by the local public school to talk to the guidance and counseling department about one of my young parishioners who has recently been in trouble. I may give instructions to the women of the parish who volunteer to teach in our C.C.D. program. It might be my turn to visit the nursing homes in the area to offer Mass and give communion. If I am "fortunate," I might even find time to spend the morning organizing altar boy lists, assigning C.C.D. teachers, working on a proposal for the parish council, and completing marriage forms or the million and one tribunal forms for helping a parishioner expedite some marriage difficulty. If I am able to spend the morning in the rectory, it seems that the telephone never stops ringing with a request to ask Father this question or to make an appointment to see Father to discuss this particular difficulty. Five or six times each morning the front doorbell will ring, and either I or the parish secretary will answer. Again, someone will have a desire as simple and warm as wanting to say "hello" and chat, as trivial as the filling out of a baptism record, or as serious as some form of confessional matter. Suffice it to say that most good intentions to spend a morning at work in the rectory are usually waylaid by the pressing cares of people who want to see Father right now.

The parish priesthood is unlike any other modern profession in the sense that people expect that Father is always there waiting for them. When he is out or too busy to see them, they are disappointed and often do not understand. People who wait days to see their doctors or lawyers and other professionals in the community are not as tolerant of their parish priests. Now I am not advocating that parish priests should become professionally removed from their people. Christ was certainly not a "professional" with a sign outside his door that listed the approved times for visiting. People came to him by day and night, when he was busy and when he was often exhausted. The presence of the parish priest is very much tied to this imitation of Christ's "laying down of his life for the flock." In the following chapter, I will speak of this difficulty more directly from the perspective of Christ's care to go apart and be by himself in prayerful intimacy with his Father.

By the time noon arrives, I am usually back at the rectory for lunch or picking up a snack at some meeting I am attending or some hospital or nursing home I am visiting. If I am eating at the rectory, I may again find that I am eating alone, for my associate has the day off and the pastor is attending a luncheon get-together. In a modern busy parish, priests who live together are very often like ships passing in the night. The one time that they may be physically together in the household is when they are asleep. Often there is no time to be together personally because there are so many day-to-day demands, so much to work on and do constantly. I may find that I turn to a newspaper or magazine to kill this time of being alone while eating my sandwich. On the table next to me there are likely to be three or four notes telling me that certain people have called and would like to talk to me or make an appointment to sit down to chat. Within a few minutes I usually find myself on the phone calling these same people and setting up appointments in an already overstuffed appointment book.

Halfway through this attempt to catch up with people who are attempting to catch up with me, I find that it is 1:00 P.M. and the front doorbell is ringing. The secretary pokes her head into the kitchen where I am hurriedly making my phone calls or she rings by buzzer to let me know that a woman is here to see me. From one to three o'clock I may see two or three parishioners about problems that are troubling them. By 3:30 P.M. I am usually back on the road visiting the parish sick in our two local hospitals, visiting the local court to talk to the probation officer about one of my young friends, stopping by the local school or playground to chat with the young people, making an appearance at the storefront information center, trying to make home visitations to those who have recently moved into the parish, or stopping by to say hello to people who have not been visited by a priest in years.

At about 5:30 P.M. I return to the rectory and, if there is any time between arrival and supper at 6:00 P.M., I will try to squeeze in a hurried breviary reading which is far removed from an attentive praying. At supper time I may be joined by the pastor and one or both of my fellow curates and, for the first and probably the last time in my daily rhythm, I will have a chance to be myself with my co-workers. The interesting thing is that so often the milieu is not conducive to being oneself. Each of us is so often preoccupied with problems and questions that have arisen during the day, or with plans and policies for the future, that we do not really give ourselves the time and space to relax genuinely and enjoy one another's company. We may talk "shop." If I have a favorite project, I may be scheming how best to propose my idea in order that it will be well accepted rather than rejected. In a busy parish each of us has his own responsibilities and, consequently, there is a tendency to want selfishly to preserve one's investment. Our lives and our cares are often scattered in isolation from one another. Oftentimes we can mistrust the motives of one another and become defensive in one another's presence. The "boss" or pastor may be someone we try to get around. Often we do not face issues together but instead try to keep everyone superficially happy by not rocking the boat. If the relationships among us are too threatening, we will not even talk "shop" but merely pass the time by talking about superficial things such as the weather, current news, or a sports event. We may become masters of talking in order to talk, but we may never really talk about our true concerns, never really dare to care enough to share our real persons.

In a way, we can be the living contradiction of Saint Paul's beautiful analogy of the Mystical Body. In subtle and manipulative ways, I say to my fellow priests, "Well, I'm an eye and I see; I don't need you, for you are just a hand." At the same time the priest who is the hand is saying, "Yes, that's right, I am a hand and you are an eye; I don't need you." The pastor at the same time might be saying, "Well, isn't that interesting; I'm the head, and I say to you, feet, I do not need you." We forget those insightful and challenging words of Saint Paul when he wrote:

> Just as a human body, though it is made up of many parts, is a single unit because all these parts, though many, make one body, so it is with Christ. . . . Nor is the body to be identified with any of its many parts. . . . Instead of that, God put all the separate parts into the body on purpose. If all the parts were the same, how could it be a body? As it is the parts are many but the body is one. The eye cannot say to the hand, "I do not need you," nor can the head say to the feet, "I do not need you. . . ." God has arranged the body so that more dignity is given to the parts which are without it, and so that there may not be disagreements inside the body, but that each part may be equally concerned for all the others. If one part is hurt, all parts are hurt with it. If one part is given special honor, all parts enjoy it.

> (1 Cor. 12:12-26)

At the conclusion of a supper get-together at which, for the most part, we are not genuinely and honestly there or personally present with each other, it is 6:30 P.M. and time to catch up on the day's news on television. At 7:00 P.M. each of us goes his separate way. The pastor might moan to himself and to us that this is the evening for the parish council to meet in order to tell him how to run "his" parish. He lets us know who the trouble makers are who want to take over the church. With those trusting and charismatic words echoing like tinkling cymbals in my ears, I find myself sitting in one of the rectory offices staring into the eyes of one of those "trouble makers" who does not want to take over the parish but who sincerely wants to know more about his or her faith. After an hour of religious instruction with this person, I may have the pleasure of sitting with a young couple who have come to make arrangements for their wedding. Then again, I may find myself embroiled in some family or marriage difficulty. At nine o'clock I may choose to attend the final rounds of the parish council meeting and hear open admissions or whispered confidances that the pastor and his priests do not trust or understand the goodwill of those who have volunteered their time to help "our" parish grow. I may choose to attend the weekly Alcoholics Anonymous meeting in the parish basement and talk with people who are trying to find their way back to sanity. I may drop into a parish discussion group or decide to stop in and visit with a family who has just lost a loved one and needs more than just the hurried prayers and condolences of their parish priest at an evening's wake services.

Finally, I find myself trudging up to my room about 11:30 or 12:00 P.M. I am completely exhausted, and I do not know where my day has gone. I have hardly found any time to relax and be myself. I have not enjoyed the brotherly friendship, assistance, or support of my fellow priests. I have scarcely been able to pray to the Lord. In my tiredness, I say to myself, "Well, that's the way it is. I chose this life and there's no sense in griping. It's all for the Lord, and I'm sure that he understands what a crazy rat race I live in. He will give me the grace to continue and so I bet-

ter get some shut-eye before it all begins again tomorrow morning.'' As I fall into bed, I notice that I am experiencing more and
more difficulty getting to sleep. I want to sleep, but I am so
wound up from problems and concerns of the day that weigh
heavily that I am unable to drop off. I look at my desk in the
darkness, and I see it as just an indistinguishable pile of papers,
notes, books, and records. My floor is littered with more un-
finished signs of a person who just does not have enough time
and space in his life to catch up. I have no time, no space in my
life that is not given over to working for souls. I feel like a
prisoner in my own parish. My rectory is not a home but just
another place to work. I am on call twenty-four hours a day, and
at any moment I can be awakened from sleep to rush off to the
emergency room of the local hospital to anoint the dying or to
console a family that has just lost a beloved member to some
tragedy.

Mine is the ordinary rhythm of the parish priest. The altar boy
who innocently asks me after Mass what I do all day besides say
Mass believes, I am sure, that celebrating Mass is all I do. When
I was an altar boy, I probably filled in my own answer to the
question of what a priest's life is like with the same romantic
thoughts that Father Hugh Kennedy had in Edwin O'Connor's
novel, *The Edge of Sadness:*

> I think of a single scene I once saw in a moving picture,
> many years ago. It was a scene in which a priest was walking
> alone at night, through a district which I'm sure was intended
> to be very much like this one. It was sordid enough, suitably
> down at the heels, yet in the film it had an odd liveliness: one
> had the impression of neon and noise and motion. There was a
> peculiar wailing music in the background, and from the
> darkness came an occasional scream of violence. Through the
> shadows one could see the tottering and seedy drunks, the
> faded street-walker, the few sharp-eyed hoodlums. And then
> the priest appeared: an erect man with a steady stride. He was
> quite handsome. He was also a familiar and impressive
> neighborhood figure. Although his coat collar was turned up,
> he was recognized at once; the recognition produced a chain
> reaction of edifying behavior. The drunks managed to

straighten themselves and tug respectively at their hats; the street-walker, suddenly ashamed, turned away, pointedly fingering the medal at her throat; the hoodlums vanished in their evil Cadillac; the cop on the beat relaxed for the first time, twirled his night stick happily, and hummed. . . .

The "padre" was passing by, and the district was the more wholesome for his presence. As for the "padre" himself, he continued to walk forward as strongly as ever, something about him managing to suggest, however, that he was in a dream—a muscular dream. His smile was compassionate but powerful: one had the feeling that here was a mystic from some ecclesiastical gymnasium, a combination of Tarzan and Saint John of the Cross. A saint, but all man. . . .

This ludicrous Disney-person, provoking these electric responses: all right. Or rather, not all right, but at least expected. Any priest in any movie is almost by definition a parody. Which in a way is understandable enough. I don't think many people know very much about priests—I'm not talking now about anything so complicated as the psychology of the religious, or the motives for vocation; I mean just the ordinary simple matter of how priests live from day to day, how they fill in their idle hours.[2]

Father Kennedy knew, however, that the stereotyped image of parish life and the romantic but unreal model of the parish priest was far from the truth. The ordinary life of the parish priest is much different. As I lay in my bed trying to fall asleep, I thought of Father Hugh's friend Father John Carmody who probably expressed my exhausted feelings better than anyone else when he said:

"I'm tired," he said. "Bone-tired. Exhausted. Drained dry. I feel as if a thousand suction pumps had been working over me. How about you? Aren't you tired?[3]

Yes, I am tired, so tired and filled up with a complete day of work that I cannot sleep. I begin to remember more clearly the tragic figure of Father John Carmody, the fictional priest who

---

2. Edwin O'Connor, *The Edge of Sadness* (Boston, MA: Little, Brown and Co., 1961), pp. 104-105. All material in this and subsequent chapters is reprinted with permission of Little, Brown and Company in association with the Atlantic Monthly Press. Copyright © 1961 by Edwin O'Connor
3. Ibid., p. 93.

spoke so eloquently of the growth of discontent in the lives of so
many overworked priests:

> No growth. Of any kind. Unless you mean a growth of discon-
> tent, which must be mutual now. Although I see no sign of it
> on their part; they keep coming. They won't quit. Everyday, I
> get up, I walk across to the Church, I say Mass—and that's the
> end of the day for me. Because then they begin to come in.
> Good God in heaven, how can people talk so much? It's
> endless, Hugh. Endless, endless, endless. My day is spent in
> listening to one continuous supplicating whine. I know
> everything they are going to say before they open their
> mouths: over and over again, the same troubles I've heard for
> thirty years, the same complaints, the same banalities, the
> same gossip, the same trivialities, and if you're foolish enough
> to respond, to actually offer the advice they claim they need so
> badly, they almost go crazy with impatience. Because you've
> interrupted them; they haven't finished complaining; "Yes,
> yes, Father, that's true, that's very true, but there is one thing
> more, there's one thing more I've got to tell you. . . ." There's
> always one thing more. Every day. The same old whimpers
> and whispers and groans and tears from people who can't
> manage their own lives and who can't wait to bolt down their
> breakfasts before rushing up to the rectory to tell me they
> can't. And it's all nonsense; it means nothing. I'm a priest, not
> a wastebasket. These people who every morning sing to
> themselves, "pack up your troubles in your old kit bag and
> take them to Father"—I want them for once, just once, to stay
> at home. Or at least to stop talking. To shut up. That's all.
> Just for awhile. Because I'm tired, Hugh. Dead tired. Worn
> thin. It can't go on this way.[4]

ALIENATION

When I let myself become tired and completely drained or
dry, people are no longer souls filled with the mysterious
presence of God. They become interfering problems that suck
out the last remaining breath of life. In giving all my time and
space to the care of working for my people, I no longer have
time and space to let someone care for me, least of all care for
myself. But I too am a human being. I have all the same human

---

4. Ibid., p. 409.

weaknesses and needs that require healing presence as do my people. I too need to be cared for. If I do not recognize what is happening to my life, if I let myself become totally imprisoned within the cultural myth of being the busy priest, then it is very possible and almost predictable that into my functionally oriented life will creep the edge of sadness.

When this harbinger of quiet desperation begins to creep into my life, I will find it easier to grow more impersonal in order to cope with the anxious pressure that begins to tear away at my every fiber. I will have a tendency to lose myself in the theological perspective of offering a ministry that becomes more *ex opere operato* to the neglect of the personal dimension of *ex opere operantis.* I will become the moral, sacramental, and organizational technician. A creeping cynicism and suspicion will take over, and, slowly but surely, I will close myself off to a healthy openness to my future. Rather than being the hopeful prophet of "Good News," I will more and more become stuck in today's ways as the safe and secure repetition of yesterday.

I will hide in the administration of juggling dollars and cents in order to keep the church afloat. How much money we gather together in the collection basket may begin to take priority over the gathering together of God's people. The secretary will receive orders that Father is too busy to see anyone today. Father will take more time off and attempt to find relief in outside activities. The golf score will come down, trips will be extended, fellow priests will be shunned or ignored. On the parish scene, Father will grudgingly listen to confessions but no longer hear the tortured and weary soul beneath the sins, the sinner whom God loves so much. Father will preach but what he will say will be dry and sterile, for he is no longer personally present. People will hear the words but recognize that the real person is missing. Yes, Father will be going through the motions, for he is not really there with his people any more. Each time the phone rings, Father will feel interrupted and hope that one of the other priests will answer. He will hope that one of the other priests will attend the wakes, offer the funeral services, marry the young couples, talk to the children in school, answer the parlor calls. Father will manage to find many new excuses to miss the various parish meetings, for he no longer is willing to share himself and call forth the various gifts and talents that God has entrusted to his care in the lives and experiences of his people.

When I move away from personally caring for my people in a balanced and genuine way, I cannot fool myself. I begin to know that they know. I begin to sense that the sheep no longer hear my voice nor the voice of the Lord in my priesthood. I have lost my concern for my sheep. I am no longer willing to lay down my life for them. My people no longer follow the stranger who lives in their midst. They begin to follow the other priests in the parish. I become envious and jealous, suspicious and critical of my fellow priests. Our relationship becomes edgy and anxious. My associates learn to tolerate the priest who no longer cares because he is too tired, too broken. Prayer for such a man becomes nearly impossible, and life becomes unbearable.

IDEAL SELF VS. REAL SELF

Some might say, as I have often said to myself, "Yes, this might be so in the lives of others, others who are not as strong and as well adjusted as I, but in my own life, never!" When I meet a tired priest, a priest who has become an alcoholic, a priest who has become a victim of depression, one who lives a fun-filled and free from responsibility type of escapism, another who is rigidly inflexible and authoritarian, I think it might be good to ponder whether all these types and many more were ordained that way. The answer is, for the majority, no, they were not. Surely there have been ordained priests who might have been much better off having pursued a different vocation in life. There have been other priests who have "escaped" into the priesthood. But the vast majority of priests in the history of our

American dioceses have been ordinary and very normal men. Our American malaise as diocesan priests has been and still is often due to the fact that we have encouraged and formed men to care too much. They have cared to the point of burning themselves out. I believe a priest like O'Connor's Father Kennedy is typical of what commonly eats away at the foundation of the American priesthood. Father Kennedy became an alcoholic. He could just as easily have become an absentee pastor or priest exhibiting many of the same characteristics of alienation that I have described. His alcoholism only throws into relief an Achilles' heel that is present in so many parish priests: the tendency to let an ideal self-image of the perfect worker priest destroy reality.[5]

If the modern American parish priest is guilty of anything, it might be that he has often tried too hard. If we were to ask why he tries too hard, why he cares too much even to the point of burning himself out and making himself ineffective, it might be that he has not integrated his life around his real self. I am suggesting at this point that one of the greatest tragic flaws in American priests probably is their tendency to be idealists. Now there is nothing wrong in having ideals. However, when I construct my whole life on an ideal rather than a real vision, I am inclined to lose my balance. In the unpublished thesis of which this chapter is a part, I discussed quite extensively the meaning and influence an ideal self-motivation can have on a person.[6] When my ideal self becomes the dominating factor in my being present in the world, then I usually become tyrannized by a whole constellation of ideal "shoulds." I "should" say yes to every request of my parishioners. I "should" never say no. I "should" be the perfect counselor, the perfect liturgist, the perfect youth

5. An enriching work on the true soul of the parish priest's apostolate can be found in Dom Jean-Baptiste Chautard's *The Soul of the Apostolate* (Trappist, KY: Abbey of Gethsemani, Inc., 1946).
6. Refer to *Personal Care and Pastoral Presence,* pp. 48-56, wherein I discuss Karen Horney's explanation of the ideal self vs. the real self.

director, the perfect chairman of the parish council, the perfect organizer. When my ideal self holds the upper hand, then I must always be in control, never weak, never in need, never soft or warm. I "should," I "must," I "have to" live up to the great expectations that my ideal self imposes upon my life.

I am unable to recognize or accept that I am only a limited and imperfect person. I find it difficult to accept that one day has only twenty-four hours or one week only seven days. I demand more time, more days to continue my expansive mastery over my world. I find it almost impossible to be open and surrendering. My ability to trust is almost negligible. I must always be in control, always manipulating others to get my cause accepted or accomplished. I can no longer tolerate imperfection and weakness in those around me. I am impatient when everything is not done "yesterday." My ideal self projects an impossible perfection onto myself and others. In my personal interactions, I tend to move quite rigidly and inflexibly toward, against, or away from others.[7]

Very simply my ideal self becomes my "being like god" existence. I succumb as Adam succumbed. I unconsciously turn my broken nature into a self-glorification. I hide my nakedness as a wounded son of Adam and try to find a safe and secure way in my own blueprint for life. Rather than being open or surrendering, I willfully force myself on life. If a person comes to me with a problem, then I "should" have an answer. Therefore, I will force answers, make answers, oversimplify complex issues, and produce solutions. Mystery has no place in my ideal scheme. I live by calculating and analyzing life to the point of reducing it to a safe and predictable certainty. I become the center of the world.

The ideal self can begin very early in my priesthood, as Father Hugh Kennedy testifies to in *The Edge of Sadness.* In reflecting

---

7. Refer to *Personal Care and Pastoral Presence,* pp. 48-50, in which I discuss the movement of the ideal self.

on the sadness that crept into his life and caused his depression and alcoholism, he says:

> I found an answer. It was an answer which began back in those early active years, back with the new parish hall, the improved church grounds, the spick-and-span school band, the bridge evenings for the women, the weekly gatherings of men, the outings, the school plays—all those things of which I'd always been so proud, and to which I'd given so much time. And suddenly, there was the clue before me: the "so much time." So much time that there had been no time for anything else, and I saw now, in a flash of long postponed revelation, and with a sense of shock and dismay how little the unimportant had become important for me, how those things which belonged properly on the edges of my life had in fact become the center. The young priest, without realizing it, had become little more than a recreation director: a cheerleader in a Roman collar.

> And it had been so easy, so innocent. There are, after all, certain social duties which a priest has toward his parishioners, and if that priest is as I was—energetic and gregarious, with an aptitude for such occasions—these duties and occasions have a way of multiplying. There's a great attraction to this: he's doing what he likes to do, and he can tell himself that it's all for the honor and glory of God. He believes this, quite sincerely, and he finds ample support for such belief: on all sides he's assured that he is doing the much-needed job of "waking up the parish." Which is not a hard thing for a young priest to hear; he may even see himself as stampeding souls to their salvation.

> What he may not see is that he stands in some danger of losing himself in the strangely engrossing business of simply "being busy"; gradually he may find that he is rather uncomfortable whenever he is not "being busy." And, gradually too, he may find fewer and fewer moments in which he can absent himself from activity, in which he can be alone, can be silent, can be still—in which he can reflect and pray. And since these are precisely the moments which are necessary for all of us, in which spiritually we grow, in which, so to speak, we maintain and enrich our connection with God, then the loss of such moments is grave and perilous.

> Particularly so for a priest—particularly for a priest who

suddenly finds that he can talk more easily to a parish committee than he can to God. Something within him will have
atrophied from disuse; something precious, something vital. It
will have gone almost without his knowing it, but one day, in a
great crisis, say, he will reach for it—and it will not be there.
And then . . . then he may find that the distance between the
poles is not so great a distance after all. . . .

   This was the answer which came to me on that morning. It
was not a consoling answer; is it ever consoling to learn that
you've been most mistaken in something of which you've been
most proud of?[8]

To be most mistaken in what you have been most proud sums up
the fundamental core of the ideal self. The same pride that
tripped up Adam, the same pride that turned the Israelites into
hardened and rebellious hearts in the desert and exile, the same
pride that left the Pharisees with eyes that no longer saw and
ears that no longer heard the Good News of Christ, this same
pride lives as the self-inflating energy behind the ideal self.

   In the parish priesthood, power can corrupt just as it can in
any other form of leadership position. At the Last Supper,
Christ washed the feet of his disciples, for he knew what lurked
in the heart of man:

   If I, then, the Lord and Master, have washed your feet, you
   should wash each other's feet. . . . I tell you most solemnly no
   servant is greater than his master, no messenger is greater than
   the man who sent him.

                                                    (John 13:14-16)

   No, the greatest among you must behave as if he were the
   youngest, the leader as if he were the one who serves. For who
   is the greater: the one at table or the one who serves? The one
   at the table, surely? Yet here am I among you as one who
   serves!

                                                    (Luke 22:26-27).

The whole mystery of Christ's care for souls entrusted to him by
his Father was real because it was rooted in the reality of humble
service. Paul put it magnificently when he wrote: "His state was

---

8. O'Connor, pp. 135-36.

divine, yet he did not cling to his equality with God but emptied himself to assume the condition of a slave" (Phil. 2:6-7).

ANXIETY PROPHESIES MY BEING-UNTO-NOTHINGNESS

Why am I so inclined to become a functional man? Why am I inclined to construct an ideal self that attempts to hold on to life and works for its self-glorification? Martin Heidegger captures this question at a fundamental level when he considers the reality that man is always shadowed by his utmost possibility, his being-unto-nothingness, or death.[9] As a human being, I am a transcendent neediness. I am neither self-sufficient nor the ultimate and adequate answer to my existence as question. I am anxious. Christ understood my situation clearly when he told the parable of the rich man and Lazarus who was poor. When the rich man asks Father Abraham to send a messenger into the world to warn his surviving brothers about the afterlife, Abraham replies: "If they will not listen either to Moses or the prophets, they will not be convinced even if someone should rise from the dead" (Luke 16:31). Shakespeare expresses the same idea in *Hamlet*:

> To be, or not to be: that is the question.
> . . . .
> But that the dread of something after death,
> The undiscover'd country from whose bourn
> No traveller returns, puzzles the will
> And makes us rather bear those ills we have
> Than fly to others that we know not of?
> Thus conscience does make cowards of us all. . . .[10]

No one of us realistically speaking rests easily with the mystery of death. It is easier to believe that someone else will die than to believe that such an experience will befall ourselves. The actual facing of death as the utmost boundary of life is often

---

9. Refer to *Pastoral Care and Pastoral Presence,* pp. 40-42, in which I discuss Martin Heidegger's consideration of man's moodedness in anxiety and his being-unto-death.

10. *The Complete Works of William Shakespeare* (New York, NY: Halcyon House, 1964), III, i, 56 and 79-83.

postponed or escaped. It is easier, then, for us to let ourselves become tranquilized by the anonymous crowd consciousness that lives the illusion that death can be covered over. In order to belong to the flattering mediocrity of the crowd, to refuse to become the single one who emancipates himself or herself from the crowd in order to take full responsibility for his or her real life, it is necessary to follow the blind leveling-down process of being the average person. For a priest this leveling means thinking like "they" think, desiring what "they" desire, acting like "they" act.

I can accept the ideal ethic of the crowd, which suggests that to get ahead, to belong in this highly competitive society, one must work. The crowd may also offer other ideal images of belonging such as "not working," being "fun-filled and irresponsible," "living off others" and so on.[11] Some priests may choose these more dependent ideal images and dry up and become sterile through living a life of complete irresponsibility. The important point is that the ideal mode of life becomes a way to cope with the threatening anxiety of not being able to face comfortably my being-unto-nothingness. The ideal crowd ethic I choose may be the ethic of a clerical culture that demanded personal perfection in seminary training. On the other hand, the crowd may be a rebellious subculture within the wider clerical culture that reacts indifferently or in an angry way to the model of perfection. Then again, the crowd may be the wider culture of everyday life in the world.

In an ideal way of living, I will hold on for dear life to the secure and safe world I know and can manage so well. To reflect on the mystery of death as it touches my life is too risky. It smacks of the unknown, the transcendent, the unwelcome. I prefer to hang on to my "little beyonds." Because the mystery

---

11. Refer to Soren Kierkegaard's work, *The Present Age* (New York, NY: Harper & Row, 1962), which is a brilliant exposure of the false ideals and ways of the crowd.

of death lies in my future, I begin to shut myself off from the future. I snuggle safely into the cozy and well-worn paths of my past. The future is too risky. It faces me toward the hour of my death. It invites me into an experience of not knowing. It invites me to die to my old self and to rise again to real life.

Interestingly enough, I can get up on a pulpit and preach about the eschatology of the last things. I can preach words that attempt to offer hope and resurrection in Christ. I can talk endlessly about the renewal of the church in the future, but if I have not truly faced death as a reality for me, then I have not faced the fundamental reality and poverty of my life. I have merely preached the paschal mystery while having failed to live it. When old Charlie Carmody is dying in O'Connor's novel, he says:

> "A man likes to know the time . . . ." There was more silence. Then he said suddenly and loudly, "I hate to go. I hate it like the devil. They talk about dying happy: it's all bunk. There's no such thing as dyin' happy. Don't believe them when they tell you that one, Father. They talk about heaven. All right: I got nothing against that. I know there's a heaven and I hope to God I wind up there, but the thing is this, Father: who wants to wind up there now? I got my plans all made; I still got things to do. How can a man die happy if he's got things like that on his mind? How can a man do that? All right, I'll go because I got to go, and I hope I have good luck wherever I go, but I tell you this, Father: I'd a damn sight rather stay here. Where I know what's what."[12]

Charlie's loved ones react to his dying thus:

> This is a hard time, always, for those who are waiting—and it's harder, of course, the more intimately you're involved. Silence, I suppose, might be to some purpose at such a time, but in actual fact it's impossible: everyone feels compelled to say something—assurances, unconvincing optimism, leaden consolations. Whatever one says is likely to be fitful, forced, highly repetitive; everyone is aware of simply marking time . . . .[13]

---

12. O'Connor, p. 352.
13. Ibid., p. 333.

The face of death, because it is the final doorway into the transcendent mystery, causes all men to be anxious. Even Christ himself cried in sorrow at the death of his friend Lazarus. He cried in agony in Gethsemane at the vision of his own death when the final drops of his humanity would have to be shed in obedience to the will of his Father. But Christ did not turn away. He did not turn back. He accepted the chalice of suffering. He came to his hour. He did not climb down from the cross. Christ faced his death. The whole movement of the Gospels is the movement of Jesus toward his death.

To face my death is to realize that, ultimately, I cannot hang on to life. I cannot go back. I cannot escape the utmost possibility of my life. To face my death as real is to accept myself as real. It is to accept that there is a "beyond me" that I cannot control, that I cannot manage. I am always a being unto a reality beyond my experience. I cannot find anyone who has come back from death to tell me what it is all about and to put my mind at rest. Old Charlie Carmody put it well when he said, "I'd a damn sight rather stay here. Where I know what's what." Knowing what is what is another way of saying, "I know how to handle day-to-day life. I can hold on. I can stay on top and in control." I can construct all kinds of barns to store my taken-for-granted ways of knowing and living and forget that Christ, in relating the parable of the rich man, said, "Fool! This very night the demand will be made for your soul; and this hoard of yours, whose will it be then?" (Luke 12:20).

One would imagine that priests would naturally have made their peace with the mystery of death. Again, maybe this belief is one of the romantic myths of the priesthood that could benefit from a bit more honest and humble demythologizing. Priests are human like everybody else, and death and the existential anxiety that accompanies it shadow their existence as much as they shadow those of any other person. To be sure, the parish priest is constantly in the arena with death. But he is more like an observer watching death happen to somebody else. He can conduct four funeral services in a week's time and a hundred or so funerals in a year and become coldly efficient and mechanically indifferent. Death is something he takes care of, another problem that has to be handled, another service that he does. But where is the real person? Has the parish priest let himself be open to the real possibility of death as the over-arching boundary of his own life? Is he open to being touched by death in his own person? This is a serious question, and only each individual priest can answer it in the inner recesses of his heart. In facing one's death, one may for the first time situate oneself in one's true reality of dependent creaturehood. One may begin to discover the vision of true spiritual poverty, enabling one to see and live through the masks and disguises of one's ideal ways.

THE MALE MYSTIQUE

One of the interesting characteristics of the American priesthood is its exaltation and preservation of the male mystique. Parish priests can feel quite comfortable when mixing with the men and young boys of the parish. For most men, the local parish priest has arrived when he is known as "a man's man" or a "regular guy." If Father knows all there is to know about sports, he can often be a big success with the youngsters. The last thing in the world that the average parish priest would like to convey is that he is anything less than a man. These attitudes are the outcome of a clerical culture that has overly protected priests from coming to a comfortable self-acceptance of sexuality and sees women as threats to integral virginity. Women were those mysterious creatures that seminary spiritual directors warned young priests to keep at an extraordinarily safe distance. In a Cartesian kind of way, the formation years were dedicated to stressing inner holiness to the exclusion of what it means to stand out in the world as a whole person. In a spirituality that was highly dualistic, the body, the emotions, the natural drives of man were suspect. The life of a disembodied spirit perfectionism was stressed. Because the priest was called to a celibate state in the Western Church, any real contact with women on the level of intimate friendship was excluded.

After many years of isolated training in seminaries in which the whole day-to-day rhythm was one of being closely locked up in a totally male environment, it is not surprising that many priests find interpersonal relations with the women of their parish a difficult task. Women were that other half of the human race who in seminary indoctrination did not seem to arrive at full equality with men. Because so many priests do not have a comfortable integration with the feminine character and, in fact, are insecure in their own sense of a well-defined and stable acceptance of their masculinity, there is a tendency to overcompensate by being dominantly male-oriented. This way of being in the world can often be aggressive, insensitive, expansive, coldly efficient, highly functional, and duty- and goal-oriented.[14] One can sense a great deal of threatened defensiveness with the feminine modality, which is a way of standing out in the world by dwelling with and tending to essential values. I do not mean to infer that priests are not value-oriented. Rather, I am suggesting that often they will be more inclined to act aggressively in their world than to dwell openly with it at a deeper level. If I am uncomfortable with my own sense of masculinity, it follows quite naturally that I will want to prove myself. One of the ways to prove myself is to overexaggerate a linear movement or horizontal involvement with my world. I may become so "busy" that I have no time and space to root myself in a deeper richness of life.

In the masculine mode, I will have the tendency to project a world of hardness and stubborn resistance. The masculine world

---

14. Refer to *Personal Care and Pastoral Presence,* pp. 76-80, wherein I discuss F. J. J. Buytendijk's consideration of the masculine and feminine modes. Refer also to pp. 78-79, in which I discuss in footnote #25 Erikson's explanation of the masculine and feminine modes.

is a practical kind of world in which reality is simply "there." It is opposed to a feminine mode, which might be more inclined to project a world of softness and warmth, a world without stubborn resistance, a world that might possibly be "here," for it lives with the unconditional faith that hidden values have the possibility of being realized. The "stubborn" parish priest who knows practically what is good for "his" parish at all times is not an uncommon phenomenon. The parish priest who understands the duties and obligations of the faith and strongly commands obedience to all kinds of non-negotiable laws and parish policies is not unusual either. An authoritarian type personality can take over. Such a priest will have little inclination to act autonomously, to think deeply about himself, or to admit his own inner feelings. He will ironically be dominated by a desire for dominance over others and an excessive wish to maintain order and system in his own affairs. Rather than free and serve his people, he will tend to manipulate and control them. He may become highly judgmental about moral rightness or wrongness by safely standing at a distance and looking at behavior from an objective and outside viewpoint. His underdeveloped person may make it almost impossible for him to enter into the troubled and disordered world of the other in a deeply caring and sharing way, to wear somebody else's skin for a while.

The parish priest who lives the model of the army general who barks orders and keeps people at a safe distance in fear and trembling is far removed from the warm and inviting presence of Christ. Life in many parishes is like stepping into a giant deep freeze storage locker in which there is no semblance of warmth and the only ones who may be "close" to Father are a few male confidants, either laymen or possibly priest cronies who make up the weekly foursome in golf. As one "successful" old pastor put it to me when I was newly ordained, "Father, you must understand that the Church is not a playground. It is more like an army. I am the general and you young curates are my lieutenants. We can't allow confusion, disrespect, or subversion among the troops. Learn to keep a safe distance from the people. They don't know where they are going and so we must be ready at all times to tell them what is allowed and what isn't. It takes courage to be a strong leader like this." Fortunately, I smiled and left his parish "headquarters" and, I hope, went out to minister to God's people as a servant.

I cannot be overly critical of such a priest, for in my own life I can discover some of these same hard characteristics. In fact, most priests can. It is many times easier to give orders than to listen to the Holy Spirit speaking in all the people. It is not easy to admit that I can be attracted to the warm smile, the sparkling eyes, the gentle goodness, the graceful body lines of a woman, when my whole training has encouraged me to look the other way or convince myself that I am not attracted. To wait on the gifts that God has entrusted to women can often be difficult and foreign to "my ways." I cannot impose my "practical" thinking on a woman who in a certain situation may be living more from a deeply intuitive or emotional ground. I cannot always impose my experience as a man on a woman's experience as a woman. Women, in their attitudes and ways of being in the world, are oftentimes very different from me. And thank God they are! It would certainly be a dull world if it were made up only of men. The natural polarity between the sexes is not a phenomenon I must deny. It is one of God's most magnificent gifts. The real world is both male and female, and within each person the masculine and feminine modes are potentially present. In the next chapter, I will discuss further the need a priest has to integrate a more stable balance of both these qualities in his existence if he is to care for all the souls entrusted to him.

LONELINESS

In the life of the busy priest or the priest who has stopped ministering and found some other kind of escape from being truly present to his people, there is quite often a sense of profound loneliness.[15] A secular priest does not have a religious community in which to live. As one parish priest stated, "We are constantly on the front line." There is a great deal of truth to that statement. The front line is often the line of constant giving of oneself to people and their problems. The parish priest is not able to come home from work to sit down and enjoy his wife and family as can most men who leave work to come home to a dwelling separate from their places of work. The parish priest does not have the supporting affirmation of a religious community or a community house that is strictly a home separate from his work. I think it is safe to say, then, that one of the most difficult burdens of the parish priesthood is the priest's experience of loneliness. In all the feverish activity of the busy priest, in the fits of depression and melancholy that trouble some, in the tendency to drink too much to escape, in the constant hypochondria of others, in the exhausted periods of not knowing what is coming next, there is always the shadowing terror of human loneliness.

The parish priest, like everyone else, is a single individual. He is often conscious of himself as an isolated and solitary one. This awareness is often too frightening to bear, and so he runs away from the terror of being alone.[16] To be alone with himself is a taboo that he "should" avoid as much as possible. To be alone is painful and disconcerting to the "perfect one" who prides himself on having his whole life together. In a clerical culture based on a seminary formation geared to turning out "perfect" men to fill vacant slots on the assembly line of diocesan concerns, loneliness can mean that for some unknown reason, the priest has failed in his programming. He has failed to be perfect,

---

15. Refer to *Personal Care and Pastoral Presence,* pp. 160-63, in which I discuss Clark Moustakas's explanation of existential loneliness and loneliness terror.
16. Refer to *Personal Care and Pastoral Presence,* pp. 96-100, in which I discuss Adrian van Kaam's understanding of original terror.

and many times he can feel guilty at being less than the ideal model of a distorted view of sanctity. In a clerical system that prided itself on knowing all the questions about life and, consequently, all the answers, a deeper and more fundamental reality either was never faced or was rigidly ignored. That reality is the truth that man is more than just a soul split apart from his body. Man is a total unity of both body and soul. To think that a formation system could prepare a young man for ministry in the world by stressing a disembodied spiritual existence reflected a lack of vision. To pretend that a man's fundamental human condition of existential loneliness could be bypassed by stressing constant study, prayer, and busy involvement was absurd.

Unfortunately, what we sow in our lives has one day a harvest. If a young seminarian's life is not cultivated with space and time to be creatively alone with himself and with his God, then it is only natural that an experience of loneliness that can be frightening and devastating may occur later on in his life. Before any man can "do" or "have" anything in this life, he must first realize that he "is." "Doing" all kinds of activities or "having" all kinds of information certainly offers an incomplete profile of man's existence. Fundamentally, I am a unique person and, as such, I am a gift of God. God did not create me with all kinds of strings attached, strings that demand I "do" this or I "have" that. God does not place conditions on his love and his care for me. He loves me because I am. He cares for me in spite of my imperfections and weaknesses. In fact, in the life of a priest he has often, in the words of Saint Paul, "chosen the foolish to confound the wise." Now this is a difficult understanding for most priests to accept, especially when we have been brought up in a system of formation that has demanded that we be perfect. To know that I am supposed to be perfect, and yet to experience at a more honest level of my conscious awareness that I am far from perfect, is frightening. To be alone with myself is to come face to face with my limitations, with the honest reality of who I really am. In loneliness I discover the fundamental breach between what I so often pretend to be or would like to be and the person I really am. For many of us, this reality is too much to bear.

Therefore, a great deal of my life as a priest can be an unconscious and even a conscious running away from the experience of loneliness in which I must face my real self. I rescue others from loneliness because I cannot face loneliness and what it may tell me about my own life. I find it difficult to stand by lonely persons and give them a personal presence that enables them to let their loneliness be in order to commune with the insights that lie hidden in its depths. As a parish priest, it becomes more and more difficult to spend an evening alone in my rectory room, for such an experience means facing the possibility of meeting loneliness face to face. If I have time off, then I must be with priest friends or parishioners who will see to it that I am not alone. In a pathetic way, the free time of my celibate state may become filled with various ways to overcome ever experiencing myself as alone. Celibacy, which should give me time to be with myself and time to be with God in prayerful intimacy, now becomes a burden that I carry, a burden that haunts my very existence with the terror of being the lonely one.

ROLES PRIESTS PLAY

The lonely person, the ideal person, the functional person is one who cannot risk becoming open to himself. He has never truly separated himself from the world he lives in to find within himself a self-esteeming center of interior strength.[17] He finds it difficult to be himself because, in his own eyes, he is under constant pressure to be someone else. His life is not an openness to possibilities and the emergence of new and original values but

17. Refer to *Personal Care and Pastoral Presence,* pp. 88-90, in which I discuss Emmanuel Levinas's consideration of the importance of natural separation and centered living.

more a defense system that helps him cope with his original experience of separation and anxiety.[18] Eugene Kennedy talks of common games or roles priests may play.[19]

The "Laughing Boy" game describes the affable, good guy priest whose chief response in many situations is laughter. This laughter is not of joy but of a reaction to living so much on the surface of life that I am forced to make a joke even when it is the least appropriate response imaginable. The laughing modality enables me to block off any serious self-examination or examination of what is really happening in a certain situation. It can be an attempt to reassure myself that all is well, and it enables me to stay at a safe distance not only from myself but from others by cushioning my relationship with this unhealthy gaiety.

The "Parasite" game allows me to relate to my people in such a way that I can reap the rewards of their presence in my life while they get very little in return from me. I am always wangling tickets for sports events or invitations to dinner or enjoying a pleasant glow with the upper crust and the influential. The notion of the "privileges" of the priest is uppermost in this attitude. I need not stand in lines; I should be able to play golf or vacation at reduced rates or for free; I need not be ticketed when I break speed laws; I demand discounts for every purchase. I simply care to be there with my people in order to get the most out of such relationships for myself. Such a game is a failure because its rewards are ultimately empty and because it gives rise to such resentment among the people who are forced to play the game.

----

18. *Personal Care and Pastoral Presence,* pp. 99-100. Here I discuss Adrian van Kaam's explanation of an initial, uncongenial, fundamental life style that is built on reactive social patterns.
19. Material for this section on role playing is taken from Eugene C. Kennedy's work, *Comfort My People* (New York: Sheed & Ward, 1968), pp. 116-20.

In the "Expert" game, I operate by knowing all the answers to the problems of others. I know exactly what they should do in every decision of consequence. By knowing everything, I need not open myself to learn anything in my relationships with others or with myself. Slowly but surely, this phenomenon is breaking down in today's church as the mood of uncertainty grows in the lives of so many priests. However, the very fact that ambiguity and uncertainty can be so disconcerting to so many priests illustrates how strong was their previous need to be expert and right in all matters.

The "I Need to Cure You" game is related to the "Expert" game. It occurs when I am unable to face and accept my own limitations or understand that Christianity does not demand instant perfection as much as it demands constant growth. When this attitude creeps into my life, I expect to succeed, according to the goals I have set, in every situation. I can become deeply upset when I do not carry off some situation with the perfection that I demand. Of course, this game is self-defeating because I can never win it. I can never cure everybody, solve every difficulty, heal every wound, or convert every passer-by. Even Christ did not attain such unreal success. Because this is a loser's game, I will most often end up in a very disappointed and discouraged state.

The "Projection" game happens when I am unable to face my own feelings and identify them correctly and so I turn my own faults on everybody around me. I am able to criticize others safely because their faults are not mine but theirs. In such a game, the strong hostility that a priest can at times feel for himself is projected on others. When I am unable to accept and like myself because of some imperfection in my nature, I will rename my self-irritation as a righteous indignation toward the sinners that surround me. I become long on harangue and short on compassion. The pulpit becomes a center of "bad news" rather than "good news." This device is self-serving because I get to express my own inner feelings and attitudes in a way that deflects attention from myself. My anger is not zeal but really an isolating defense that precludes any real, authentic growth.

The "Let's Talk About It" game happens to me when I escape into an intellectual and excessively theoretical Christianity. The subjects of this game are more often theology and liturgy, but psychology and sociology serve just as well. I build my life on the premise that if I talk about these subjects I have really done something about them. Maybe that is why there are so many discussion groups on the subject of Christian love, for it is safer to talk about love than to give one's own imperfect self in genuinely trying to love some other person. This is the game that becomes replete with catch-words, "in" jokes, and superficial scholarship. It is a refuge that helps me keep my distance from life by talking about it rather than daring to live it.

The "Love Them and Leave Them" game relates to the personalist emphasis of our present age of renewal. It is a game in which I manipulate others in order to satisfy my own needs. It combines many of the attitudes of the above games. I can, for example, be a parasite and intellectualizer as I move into the lives of others on a deep personal basis and then drop the other when the going gets rough. This happens in many relationships between priests and women. The woman is seen as a means of identifying oneself as a full-blooded male. Such a game speaks of the uneasiness many American men feel with regard to their own sense of virility. At heart, this attitude is a cold and calculating manipulation of others for my own sake. I can justify running from the other when things get difficult or too hot on the grounds that I am preserving my priesthood, and yet I never need confront or face myself and the feelings that led me into such intimate experience in the first place. I may reject an opportunity to grow and work through a responsible relationship to the other.

These games arose in a clerical culture when men were not allowed to feel free to bring their real selves into relationship with others precisely in and through their priesthood. The rules of these games were devised in an age when rules rather than values of real life were thought to be of paramount importance. In a church that has moved very quickly away from a tradition-directed and inner-directed social conditioning to a more other-directed form of being present in the world, there are still many vestiges of this gamesmanship present in our lives.[20] We are certainly living in an age that could be called the age of personal spiritual renewal, but we are foolish men if we think that we have entirely eliminated our facticity in games priests play to stay in control and preserve safe distances from people.

RESENTMENT

Max Scheler points out that resentment is a self-poisoning of the mind, for it is a lasting mental attitude caused by the systematic repression of certain emotions and affects which, as such, are normal components of human nature.[21] When repression exists in my life, I tend to indulge in certain kinds of value delusions and corresponding value judgments. The emotions and affects that are primarily involved are revenge, hatred, malice, envy, and the impulse to detract and be spiteful. Resentment arises when these emotions are particularly powerful and yet must be suppressed because they are coupled with the feeling that I am unable to act them out, either because of weakness, physical or mental, or because of fear. Whenever I continually have to hide my inner feelings and keep my negative and hostile emotions to myself, I can fall victim to resentment.

One of the great forces that lies beneath resentment is the need

20. Refer to *Personal Care and Pastoral Presence,* pp. 139-44, in which I discuss David Riesman's explanation of the tradition-, inner-, and other-directed societies in his book, *The Lonely Crowd.*
21. Material for this section is taken from Max Scheler's work, *Ressentiment* (New York: Schocken Books, 1961), pp. 43-78. Refer also to Adrian van Kaam's work, *Envy and Originality* (Garden City, NY: Doubleday and Co., 1972).

in most men to make comparisons between themselves and others. Each of us, whether we be noble or common, good or evil, continually compares his own value with that of others. The noble man, however, has a completely naive and nonreflective awareness of his own value and fullness of being. This awareness is not to be mistaken for pride. Pride, on the contrary, results from an experienced diminution of this naive self-confidence. It is a way of "holding on" to one's value, of seizing and preserving it deliberately. The noble man's naive self-confidence permits him to assimilate the merits of others in all their fullness. He does not grudge them their merits. He rejoices in their virtues. He is tuned more to the original essence and being of others. Therefore, he can afford to admit that another person has certain qualities superior to his own or is more gifted. Such a conclusion does not diminish his naive awareness of his own value, which needs no justification or proof by achievements or abilities. Achievements merely serve to confirm his value. The common man can only experience his value and that of another if he relates the two, and he clearly perceives only those qualities that constitute possible differences. The noble man experiences value prior to any comparison; the common man experiences it in and through a comparison. For the common man, every value is a relative thing, higher or lower, more or less than his own. He arrives at value judgments by comparing himself to others and others to himself.

Scheler points out two types of persons who share in this basic attitude. The strong or energetically potent person becomes an "arriviste." The ultimate value of the arriviste's aspirations is not to acquire a thing or value but to be more highly esteemed than others. He uses things as an occasion for overcoming the oppressive feeling of inferiority that results from constant comparisons. When this value system comes to dominate an entire society, then the soul of such a society becomes a system of free competition. The goal of such a competitive society becomes the need to surpass others. Such a value system does not set well with the value challenge of Christ's unselfish love.

If the personality type is impotent, the person can find relief only by the value delusion of resentment. He seeks a feeling of superiority or equality and attains it by devaluing another's qualities or by a specific blindness to such qualities. The phenomenal peculiarity of the resentment delusion can be described by saying that the positive values are still felt as such, but that they are overcast by the false values and can shine through only dimly. The resentment experience is always characterized by this transparent presence of the true and objective values behind the illusory ones. There is an obscure awareness that one lives in a sham world that one is unable to penetrate.

In the life of a priest, resentment may break out in an "old maid" prudery. Because the priest represses cravings for tenderness, sex, and propagation, he may become the victim of ferreting out all sexually significant events in order to condemn them harshly. This is sexual gratification transformed into resentment satisfaction. The criticism accomplishes the very thing it pretends to condemn. Resentment imitates genuine modesty by means of prudery.

Another situation that can affect priests is the growing resentment of the older generation toward the younger priests. The process of aging can be fruitful and satisfactory only if the important transitions are accompanied by free resignation or free renunciation of the values proper to the preceding stage of life. Spiritual and intellectual values that remain untouched by the process of aging, together with the values of the new but older age, must compensate for what has been lost. If as an older priest I cannot compensate, I will avoid and flee the tormenting recollection of youth. This avoidance and flight will block my possibilities for understanding younger people. At the same time I will tend to negate the specific values of earlier stages, and young people will find me a closed and consummate bore. The interesting thing to note is that, in a society that is undergoing the "future shock" of novelty, new changes, and transience, the average priest can experience himself growing older far before his time.[22] If he does not stay up in his studies and reflection on the new age he is living in, he can, even in his thirties or forties, show the aging symptoms that priests used to show when they moved into their senior years. Resentment can become an integral part of his way of coping with his newly experienced impotency.

Scheler points out that the priest more than any other man is liable to live with resentment. The priest often is condemned to control his emotions such as revenge, wrath, and hatred, at least outwardly. He must always represent the image and principle of peacefulness and sanctity. He can adopt a typical priestly policy of gaining victories through suffering rather than combat or confrontation. Scheler suggests that although there is no resentment in genuine martyrdom, resentment is present in false martyrdom. Of course, this observation touches one of the day-to-day realities of most parish priests' lives. When one is overworked, when one is always expected to live the role of being the perfect priest, the saint living in the midst of his people, a great deal of resentment can fester in one's life. Such a priest can become very angry and have no way to release such pent up energy.

One of the forms that resentment can take in today's church is what Scheler calls the "spiritual apostate." The apostate is motivated by the continuing struggle against his old belief and lives only for its negation. He does not affirm his new convictions for their own sake but is engaged in a continuous chain of revenge against his own spiritual past. In reality, he remains a captive of his past, and his new faith is merely a handy frame of reference for negating and rejecting the old. The apostate is at the opposite pole from the "resurrected" person whose life is

---

22. Refer to *Personal Care and Pastoral Presence,* pp. 149-53. Here I discuss Alvin Toffler's analysis of the "future shock" culture.

transformed by a new faith which is full of intrinsic meaning and value. Many of the priests who have left the church in recent times are "spiritual apostates" in Scheler's sense. Many other apostates still remain within the priesthood but continue to carry on a life style that is constantly dedicated to stamping out the old "oppressive" ways. They are able to tear down old traditions and replace them with nothing but their righteous indignation. They can witness a devoted parishioner praying a rosary at Mass and denounce such devotion as pious magic. Such an attitude says more about their own resentment level than anything important about praying the rosary at Mass. The church of recent times has endured enumerable cases of priests who have accused the past tradition of the church of being closed and authoritarian. Interestingly enough, these new apostate apostles have become just as closed and authoritarian in their crusades for updating as those they criticize.

At the parish level, this kind of resentment has caused tremendous damage to the lives and faith of simple, everyday people. Common people have been castigated from the altar for being superstitious, too docile, and too uninvolved, and they have heard a host of other angry and accusing outbursts. It is no wonder that many of these same people, who never realized that they were such arch villains or co-conspirators in such a "backward" religion, have left the church. They no longer experience a church that nurtures their faith. Many of these people have been totally disillusioned with priests who have cared more for hearing their own voices than for hearing the gentle and patient voice of the Lord. They no longer recognize the voice of such a stranger. The voice of a priest filled with resentment is the voice of a hireling who has no real concern for the flock but concern only for his own "captivity" in the past.

Resentment can break out also in a romantic nostalgia for the past that is merely a wish to escape the present. All praise of the past has the implied purpose of downgrading present-day reality. Just as the apostate attempts to put down the past in his attempt to forge a new future, the romantic puts down the present and future in his attempt to go back to the "good old days." The interesting thing is that resentment expression is always the same. The past is affirmed, valued, and praised not for its own intrinsic quality, but with the unspoken intention of denying, devaluating, and denigrating the present. The past is played off against the present. The "romanticist" will argue that the Latin Mass is the true way to celebrate the liturgy. This argument is his way of playing it off against the new reform of the vernacular liturgy. The apostate will argue in just the opposite direction. Put one priest of each type in the same rectory, and imagine the conflict that will occur. Put one of these types together with one or more well-adjusted fellow priests, and the romanticist or the apostate will constantly be a divisive influence in a common caring for the souls of the parish. Enlarge this dilemma to the priest's involvement with the people of his parish who, because they are human, can have the same energy of resentment working in their life styles, and one gets a clearer picture of the day-to-day struggle that may exist within one flock.

Finally, repressed impulses tend to radiate in all directions. My resentment turns into a negative attitude toward certain traits and qualities that trouble me no matter where or in whom they are found. When my repression is complete, the result is a general negativism or a sudden, violent, seemingly unsystematic and unfounded rejection of things, situations, or natural objects whose loose connection with the original cause of my hatred can be discovered only by a complicated analysis. In *The Edge of Sadness,* Father John Carmody is an excellent example of a repressed person who has reached the point of rejecting almost totally the life of a parish priest. Everyone and every event has become an exhausting torture in his life. Father John has never been able to face up to the dominating influence of his tyrannical father. In his father's presence, he is as docile as a lamb.

Once he is back in the parish, he is cold and lifeless, and his whole life has become a burden.

Again and again, the man of resentment encounters happiness, power, goodness, beauty, wit, and other phenomena of positive life. These phenomena exist and impose themselves, however much he may shake his fist against them and try to explain them away. He cannot escape the tormenting conflict between desires and impotence. When such a quality irresistibly forces itself upon his attention, the very sight suffices to produce the impulse of envy or hatred against its bearer who has never harmed or insulted him. Many times this "hidden agenda" can become the difficulty in broken lines of communication between priests working in the same parish. A resentment attitude can turn a parish house and an entire parish into turmoil because no one understands why Father is so unreasonably upset or why members of the same parish organization can blow their tops at each other and ruin well-laid plans. Eventually, the man of resentment cannot justify or even understand his own existence and sense of life in terms of positive values such as power, health, beauty, goodness, freedom, and independence. Weakness, fear, anxiety, and a slavish disposition prevent him from obtaining them. He comes to feel that "all is in vain anyway" and that salvation lies in the opposite extreme of poverty, suffering, illness, and death. Resentment thus turns to the final and sublime revenge against oneself. In *The Edge of Sadness*, Father John Carmody dies from internal hemorrhaging. If one wants to hold to psychosomatic conditioning, his death shows the result of outward expression that is blocked. Inner visceral sensations that accompany every affect can come to prevail. Father John was finally eaten away internally by his resentment. Father Hugh Kennedy, on the other hand, repressed the meaning of his father's death and his helplessness in the face of witnessing his father waste away. Eventually, the edge of sadness crept into his life in the form of extreme melancholic depression and consequent alcoholism. Father Hugh survived only because he finally faced himself in the loneliness of taking a cure in a home for alcoholic priests. In facing the true object of his repressed anger and frustration, he was able to liberate himself from the radiating effect resentment had had in all areas of his life.[23]

SUMMARY

In this chapter, I have examined some of the obstacles in a parish priest's daily life that hinder a more personal presence in his pastoral care. My insights have been rooted in the research of fundamental human dynamics. I have looked at a typical day in my own life as a parish priest and tried to show how a priest can become caught up in a functional way of life. Such an active and busy style of life can lead to a quiet and even desperate alienation. Very often the ideal self becomes more central than the real self. There is a need to be perfect, a need to be always in control. Anxiety often creeps into daily experience. A masculine mode of living, which is often aggressive, authoritarian, insensitive, and agitated, takes over. The loneliness of the priestly life is not faced as a creative way to deeper insight but is repressed as a terrorizing emissary of human weakness. The different roles that a priest might employ to cope with his life situation come into play. Finally, I considered the phenomenon of resentment and the tremendous impact that this dynamic can have in a priest's life.

In the next chapter, I want to explore some of the important facilitating conditions that enable the parish priest to become a more genuine and authentic pastoral presence. My observations and recommendations again flow from scholarly research, now seen in the context of priestly care in a parish setting.

---

23. An excellent autobiographical account of suppressed emotions, breakdown, and therapeutic recognition and cure is found in Rev. William J. Collins's work, *Out of the Depths* (Garden City, NY: Doubleday and Co., 1971).

FACILITATING CONDITIONS
FOR PASTORAL CARE

*Anyone who finds his life will lose it; anyone who
loses his life for my sake will find it (Matt. 10:39).*

In the preceding chapter, I have discussed the various
obstacles that can enter into the daily life situation of the parish
priest and disturb his sense of pastoral care. In this chapter, I
want to consider the facilitating conditions that enable the
parish priest to live with a deeper presence of pastoral care. I
want to begin by considering the dimensions of immanence and
transcendence as fundamental dynamics in human life.[1]

IMMANENCE AND TRANSCENDENCE

Immanence is the characteristic or modality of living or remaining within myself as subject.[2] Transcendence is the modality of rising above or beyond myself as subject.[3] Van Kaam

---

1. Material for this section is taken from Adrian van Kaam's unpublished class notes, Spring Semester, 1975, Lectures 1, 2, 7, and 10. These
lectures were given at the Center for the Study of Spirituality of the Institute of Man at Duquesne University, Pittsburgh, PA.
2. *Webster's New International Dictionary* (Springfield, MA: G. & C.
Merriam Co., 1955), p. 1,245.
3. Ibid., p. 2,689.

points out that the full human being is both immanent and transcendent. Man has, in other words, the capacity to come to closure and remain closed up within a secure and stable level of his self-emergence and the capacity to remain open to becoming more of himself, open to the possibilities of his ongoing emergence. Man is always in tension between what he is presently, his immanence, and what he may become in the future, his transcendence. This condition is so because man is fundamentally an embodied spirit. My spirit calls me forth to become my original and unique self within the horizon of all that is. There is always a relation between my emerged self and my emerging self. My emerged self is my immanent dimension, whereas my emerging self is my transcendent dimension. If I am spiritually alive, I am always transcending or going beyond my present emergence. In transcending, I am opening up all the time to new projects of life, new insights, experiences, and growth. In immanence, I incarnate or take these transcendent insights into my life, and they become part of me. They are me; they are my self as already emerged.

Van Kaam points out that I must always be aware that I may have the tendency to close off the growth of my emerging self by closing myself up in immanence. I may be inclined to fixate at what I already am and rest in my immanence and stop growing, stop transcending. My immanent self enjoys being secure and safe. It enjoys being at rest. This being the case, the great danger in my human growth is that the immanence dimension may take over in my life. The power of my immanence complex begins in infancy. As an infant, I cannot think about the difference between immanence and transcendence. I merely live this tension. The person or image in my world who represents immanence is my mother. She stays at home. She gives milk. She makes me confortable as a child. My father, on the other hand, is the image of transcendence. He goes out to work. He makes big decisions. He protects my mother and me. My mother becomes, according to van Kaam, the immanent experience and my father the transcendent experience. Now this reality is tremendously important for any child. Both images appeal to basic dynamics in me. I like to cling to my mother image. My father image calls me out because he appeals by his very being to the transcendent spiritual notion. I establish a tremendous tension between clinging to my mother and even getting angry at my father. My father is the great disturber. He intrudes in that intimacy between me and my mother. There, consequently, arises in my life an immanence complex.[4]

In adult life this tension between my immanent and transcen-

---

4. Freud calls this clinging to the mother and rivalry with the father the Oedipus complex. His consideration interprets a purely sexual conflict based on the vital instincts of man. Van Kaam builds his consideration of the immanence complex on the deeper reality of the spiritual nature of man. Van Kaam points out that the infant can get so upset with the father image as transcendent intruder that his situation can be translated normally in sexual feelings. The little child expresses its clinging to the mother in immanency, and the mother replies by stroking, by feeling, by kissing, by hugging. Van Kaam also suggests that if some people stick too much to immanence, it can become a cause of homosexuality. If the child likes the immanence in the family and does not solve this preference during the immanence complex, then he may be afraid of something new. He is unable to follow the transcendent call symbolized by the father. To be confronted sexually with the other sex is new. Clinging to the immanent might mean for some homosexuals that they are unable to go beyond their own sex. They are unable to transcend their own sex because they have never worked through a comfortable relationship to the transcendent call of their father symbol. Van Kaam also cautions that some people who stick to the immanent dimension may be inclined to become priests, brothers, and sisters. They may look to continued immanence, to being in the womb of mother Church, and to the security and safe removal from the world that priesthood and religious life may afford. Such an immanence-dominated person does not have to build a family of his own. The need to encapsulate oneself in the womb of a religious family may lead to a personality that reacts blindly and impulsively to appearances in life based only on pleasure or displeasure, on sensate reward or punishment. Reflective responsibility that allows a person to project or be open to something beyond the immediately given may be atrophied.

dent nature is always present. When my immanent dimension is central, I will tend to want to stop going beyond where I am. I will want to settle down, to retire, to take it easy, to live securely and safely in a taken-for-granted and fixated daily routine. My transcendent nature, however, tends to go beyond my immediate horizon toward a wider horizon. No matter how hard I may strive to keep my life in control, I will still have to contend with the restlessness of my deeper spirit self, which is always tending to go beyond, calling me to be more alive, calling me to further growth in self-emergence. Maturity is the recognition, acceptance, and integration of these two great forces in my life, of immanence and transcendence. If I am locked in immanence, I am incomplete, for I am closed to further possibilities of self-emergence. If I am locked in transcendence, I live a free-floating openness that is not rooted in the reality of my past and present history and conditioning as man. I am always an embodied spirit living in a concrete situation handed on to me and conditioned by my family, my culture, my educational opportunities, and my experiences. I am also an openness to my future possibilities by reason of my spirit self.

The dynamics of immanence and transcendence are found necessarily in the life of every parish priest, basically because all priests are human beings like everyone else. In the preceding chapters on the pastoral presence of the parish priest, I suggested many of the obstacles that enter into the daily rhythm of a parish priest's life. I would suggest, at this point, that each of these obstacles is caused by the immanent dimension becoming dominant and by the inability to let the transcendent dimension become a balancing appeal to further growth and self-emergence. This being the case, I would like to look at these obstacles from the perspective of the transcendent call of the spirit. The parish priest is called to live in the immanent situation of concrete daily life with himself and his parishioners as the living witness or sign of the transcendent. What then are some of the facilitating conditions that may enable him to live the balanced mystery of the immanent and transcendent dimensions as a caring pastor? This is the central question that I want to explore in this chapter.

LIFE IS MYSTERY

A functionally oriented priest has the tendency to experience life as a series of never-ending problems that must be solved when, in reality, life is a mystery. Life is God's gift. The gift of life lives within me and beyond me, and, consequently, I am called to be a wayfarer.[5] The functional model of man suggests that man is the center of the universe and that it is man who projects meaning upon his world.[6] As a pilgrim wayfarer, however, I am a receiver of meaning that already exists in my world, placed there by the generous and caring presence of God. I become inspired by the meaning of my world, the events, the people, and the things of such a world, when I learn to let go of my meaning and let God's meaning emerge. The people who journeyed to Christ in the Gospels were people who were either open or closed. To the closed or immanently dominated people, Christ's words fell on deaf ears, and his vision was not seen by blind eyes. To the open or transcendent people, Christ's whole presence was new life.

The fundamental question that a parish priest has to ask is whether he is letting himself be open to a deeper and more ultimate mystery beyond himself. When I described my day-to-day functional involvement in parish life, it was obvious that there was not sufficient time and space for letting the mystery of God's presence emerge. I was totally caught up in clinging to my work. In fact, it might honestly be said that I was immanently

5. Refer to *Personal Care and Pastoral Presence,* pp. 59-62, in which I discuss Gabriel Marcel's understanding of life as mystery and man's situation as that of a wayfarer.
6. Refer to *Personal Care and Pastoral Presence,* pp. 26-28. Here I discuss Martin Heidegger's consideration of practical concern and man's tendency to be functional.

fixated in my day-to-day work in the parish. I say this because one of the most difficult experiences in my life was to leave my parish life and become a student again. As a student at the Center for the Study of Spirituality at the Institute of Man, I found myself with all kinds of new time and space. No one rang my doorbell; no one called me on the telephone with problems to solve or to sit down and discuss. No one asked me to organize committees, speak to groups, and so on. I was living in a Passionist Monastery in Pittsburgh, completely shut off from the daily routine of parish life. This time was very difficult in my life, for I had to face the mystery of being alone with myself. In this new time and space, I had to face emerging insights that began to speak painfully of how deeply caught up I was in building my whole life on caring for others. I began to sense that the last person I had been truly caring for in my parish ministry was me.

As the months wore on in my new routine of study, prayer, and reflection, I began to sense that I could not take care of myself all alone. Gradually, I found myself taking the risk of letting go and beginning to let others enter more deeply into my life and care for me. In fact, when I first began to reflect on the writing of my thesis, I naturally thought that the direction of the thesis would be more oriented to the mystery of caring for others. I thought this way because this orientation was the immanent level that I had reached in my experience as a parish priest. The longer I stayed at the Institute, the more it began to dawn on me that I could not genuinely care for others if, first of all, I was not open to being cared for by others. Others call me back to my real self. In slowly letting others care for me, I began to sense a deeper self-esteem. The experience of acknowledging that others could and did truly care for me helped me begin to care more genuinely and warmly for myself.

In letting the other come into my life, I slowly accepted that I was not perfect. In fact, I began to discover how vulnerable and broken I really am. At first, this realization was not pleasant. In initially letting a few others come more deeply into my life and care for me, I began to sense that in their hearts and minds it was okay for me to be weak. This experience was a strange reversal for a priest who had been brought up with the ideal that the priest is the perfect one who is always expected to be strong. I am sure that people were present in my rectory and in the parish itself who were ready to care for me. I doubt, however, that I ever gave them the chance. Having recently discovered new distance in my life, I can now see that I was the biggest obstacle that prevented them from caring for me. I was closed to my fellow priests, closed to my parishioners, closed so often to my friends and family. I lived with the illusion that the priest is there to be solely the caring one for others. My constant involvement in other people's lives was a subtle way to block their becoming more deeply involved in my life. I believed that I was open to others but, in a deeper sense, I was closed to the mystery of personal care existing beyond me, waiting as offered gift in my behalf.

In letting go of my taken-for-granted world of caring for others and letting others care for me, I soon discovered that it became easier to be with myself. I was able to separate from a fixating fusion with my world of functional care for others and begin to enjoy the new space and time I now had for myself. If others could care for me, then I must be worthy of care. I must be worthwhile as I really am and not because I "should" be someone else.[7] In coming home to my real self, I could now be good to the person who has just as many human needs as anybody else in this world. It became okay to "waste time" on reading books I had always wanted to read but always felt guilty about reading in the past because such reading was not directly

---

7. Refer to *Personal Care and Pastoral Presence,* pp. 48-56, wherein I discuss Karen Horney's understanding of the ideal self vs. the real self and the tyranny of "shoulds."

oriented toward my work. I began to enjoy being alone with myself, merely relaxing and reflecting on life, taking care of myself. I found that it became easier to say no to being with others merely to be with others and avoid being alone. It became easier to say no to requests that in the past I could never refuse. I began to sense that the gift of God's goodness lives in me. To take time and space for myself meant a deeper awareness and meeting with God's mysterious presence, his care, living in my real self. My worries and anxious cares about myself were now seen in the context of a deeper horizon. I was no longer isolated within my anxious need to manage life in order to stay in control or on top of life. I began to experience that ultimately my life is not my own. It is God's precious gift. I cannot possess myself. I can only gratefully accept and enjoy the mystery of who I am and who I am called to be as resting in God's will and not in my own. My life is a stewardship over his gift to me.

When all of this began to happen in my own life as a concrete daily experience and not as some beautiful new ideal I studied, talked, or wrote about, then my personal sense of caring for others took on a new texture. I began to realize that the other to whom I was ministering was just as broken and vulnerable as I.[8] We shared a common birth in original woundedness. A congenial bond existed between us. I did not have to be able to answer the other's problems, for the other was no longer a problem. The other became more of a mystery. I found that I did not know or have to know how to "fix" people up and send them back to the assembly line of life. In fact, I began to know how little I did know. I began to see how little I did see. I began to hear how little I did hear. In this new sense of spiritual poverty, I found it easier to let the other let me know where he really was

---

8. Refer to *Personal Care and Pastoral Presence,* pp. 124-26. Here I discuss Adrian van Kaam's consideration of the gentle attitude that is based on a response to one's vulnerability. The gentle person is congenially in tune with others.

and not where I thought he was or should be. It became easier to see with the other's eyes, to hear with the other's ears, to experience life from the other's point of reference, to share in the other's life as he or she was really living it and not as I presumed or analyzed his or her life from my point of reference. The other became my master, and I began to learn what it means to be one who personally cares by following as servant, by letting the other be uniquely and originally other.

The other is, ultimately, a secret mystery wonderfully created by God and originally called to be his or her own unique self and not a self that I can impose upon him or her or willfully force in any way. In the presence of the other, when I am truly there with him or her in a deep sense of personal care, I am there as one who is learning to wait upon his guest. The other is not my property or possession in any way. I cannot manage or control him or her, for he or she is God's secret. He or she is the shekinah or the tenting place of God's mysterious dwelling in my day-to-day world.[9] I am there as caring one only in the sense of hospitably offering the invitation to the other to be who he or she really is at this present time. I am a presence because I am there with him or her in mystery as he or she really is, whether it be in happiness and joy or in sorrow and suffering. I cannot rescue people from the way they are. To do so is to be absent in my presence. The way they are is the slow and often painful unfolding of their original mystery. God calls me as parish priest to be there as faithful disciple, as one who is obedient and respectful of God's ultimate presence in the other. I am there as a humble openness to the present moment of the other, as "I," called to wait and watch, to shepherd the essential personal value of the other as "Thou." We mutually call each other out of immanence into transcendence.

---

9. Refer to *Personal Care and Pastoral Presence,* pp. 174-77 and 226-30, wherein I discuss Martin Buber's understanding of authentic dialogue and the discovery of God's "Thou" or "shekinah" living in the other.

PARISH TIME

When I look back on those exhausting days in the parish, when I had no time for myself and no time to let others care for me, I am resolved that this life style cannot be that of my future life. Some might observe that it is easy to stand at a distance from parish life and make such resolutions, that once one is on the front line, all good intentions dissolve quickly. I am fully aware of such a possibility. However, I am also fully aware that the human and spiritual sanity of the parish priest rests on the firmness of such a resolution and the high priority to find more time for himself. The attrition of parish priests has been remarkably high in recent times because men have not integrated a balanced sense of time for themselves into their parish ministry. Like Father John Carmody and Father Hugh Kennedy in *The Edge of Sadness*, they have burnt themselves out. The priest of present and future times will survive as a mature person and as a spiritual witness for his people only if he does make this commitment to time for allowing God as well as others to care for him and to time for caring for himself.

TIME FOR PERSONAL FRIENDSHIP
WITH PARISH ASSOCIATES

Priests should resolve to find suitable time in rectory living to be alone with their fellow priests in order that they may begin to enjoy one another's personal presence and not allow themselves merely to discuss the work of the parish. Such resolution means attempting to grow together as friends primarily and as fellow ministers only secondarily. It means sharing what is really going on in one's ordinary confusion and anxiety. It means finding the time to be with one's common weaknesses in another's presence and letting the other offer a friendly healing. It does not mean that one becomes an open book that lets all his hang-ups stand out in naked openness. Complete or intensive transparency can be just as bad as no transparency. Genuine friendship cannot be a willful project or a forced presence. It does realistically presuppose an affinity that may or may not be present. It is also wise to remember that a healthy friendship can never be based on a "therapeutic" relationship between people who live and work in close association, for there is not a sufficient sense of distance to preserve the unique privacy that each person needs. If I am not prudent in this regard, I may find myself becoming anxious and angry in the presence of a friend in whom I may have confided too intimately. Friends have to preserve their separate selves as well as be together. True encounter calls for being with others while at the same time preserving one's separateness.[10] Priests talk a great deal about separation that exists in society at large, but they give little reflection and attention to this phenomenon in rectory life.

Time with one another as a friendly caring presence might be as simple as being able to set time apart to go out to eat together and get away from a rectory that is always so busy. It might mean taking in a movie or a play, or together dropping in on friends who live in or outside the parish, rather than developing separate coteries that cannot be shared with others. Time for developing a stronger bond of personal friendship might involve sharing one's priest friends across the generations rather than cozily remaining with the same old cronies that one met in the seminary. Although some priests do not believe it can happen, priests, like other people, can share friendship with people who are different in many ways. In fact, genuine enrichment can occur when one's circle of friends shares many varying attitudes and experiences. Older priests can be friends with younger priests in the same rectory and vice versa if the parties to the friendship care to let the other be himself with the right to believe and act in different ways.

To be truly catholic means to live universally, not merely to

10. Refer to *Personal Care and Pastoral Presence,* p. 67, in which I discuss Adrian van Kaam's caution that authentic encounter involves being together while at the same time preserving one's separateness.

carry "Catholicism" as a label of belonging. The universal man is able to break out of the immanent closure of smug and safe ways to embrace and be transcendentally open to the unique and original ways of others. If Christ was able to say that there are many rooms in his Father's house and the Kingdom of God begins in this life, then maybe priests have to reflect seriously on the fact that, in a parish or rectory setting, each priest has a deep responsibility to care for making room for the other. Is my rectory residence, is the house of my parish people, called to be any different from my Father's house? By our baptism we are all members of Christ's family but, within that family, each lives an original way. Priests who care for one another not only preach love but live it in their daily lives. One could meditate seriously on this one question and discover a great deal of food for thought. Priests who minister together in the same parish are constantly preaching about the love and care that families should come to have for one another. However, if parishioners do not experience this witness to transcendent openness in their priests' relations with one another, then it is only natural that they cannot be condemned for sensing that their priests' lives speak louder than their words and often sound like tinkling glass and clanging cymbals.

I do not think that I can ever forget that Christ sent his disciples out into the ministry as companions: they were called not only to proclaim the good news of God's loving care but also to witness to this reality in their own daily lives. Even the strong Saint Paul enjoyed and grew in association with his missionary associates, men like Timothy and Barnabas. Can we as parish priests be any different? On the road to Emmaus the two disciples walked together and eventually broke bread together while in the company of the Lord. How is it, then, that in a rectory men can ever choose to keep the peace by going their separate ways and, in reality, living as hermits cut off from the life-giving support of personally caring for one another as friends in the Lord?

TIME TO BE WITH GOD[11]

During my daily schedule as a parish priest, I was not caring to spend too much time with the Lord. Prayer and preparation for liturgical celebration were activities I fitted in if there was any time left over from my other more pressing involvements. I convinced myself that my work was my prayer and that work was all that was necessary. Father Kennedy in *The Edge of Sadness* described my situation magnificently when he said:

> What he may not see is that he stands in some danger of losing himself in the strangely engrossing business of simply "being busy"; gradually he may find that he is rather uncomfortable whenever he is not "being busy." And, gradually too, he may find fewer and fewer moments in which he can absent himself from activity, in which he can be alone, can be silent, can be still—in which he can reflect and pray. . . . the loss of such moments is grave and perilous. . . . Something within him will have atrophied from disuse; something precious, something vital. It will have gone almost without his knowing it, but one day in a great crisis, say, he will reach for it and it will not be there.[12]

The parish priest must care to find time for absenting himself from activity. He must care to find time to be alone, to be still, to be silent, to let himself pray and reflect on his life. The busy priest is an interesting character, for no matter how busy he is, he seems to be able to squeeze time for others into his schedule. Unfortunately, the last person who often gets squeezed in is the Lord himself. The Lord always seems to be at the end of the line waiting to be seen, waiting to be heard by the feverish character who is so busy taking care of the Lord's people. The life of a parish priest is often like Shakespeare's analogy in *Macbeth:* "Life's but a walking shadow, a poor player that struts and frets

---

11. Refer to *Personal Care and Pastoral Presence,* pp. 240-42, in which I discuss Adrian van Kaam's distinction between concentrated and diffuse presence to God.

12. Edwin O'Connor, *The Edge of Sadness* (Boston, MA: Little, Brown and Co., 1961), p. 136.

his hour upon the stage."[13] The priest who constantly performs to the applause and approval of the audience out front can tragically forget the ultimate backstage horizon of God's presence. To do so is eventually "to be heard no more: it is a tale told by an idiot, full of sound and fury, signifying nothing."[14] In the life of such a priest, something very special, something precious, something vital within him will have atrophied from disuse. His people will no longer hear the voice and presence of the Lord. They will not follow a stranger, for "they do not recognize the voice of strangers" (John 10:5). The priest who no longer cares to find time for the Lord in prayer is the man who becomes the ultimate and absurd contradiction.

As I reflect, I am reminded of the many married women I have met who have complained that although everyone in the community thinks that their husbands are great men because they are so busy helping others, the tragic irony is that these men who find all kinds of time for others find no time for their wives, the one person in their lives for whom they should have been able to find time. Marriage intimacy breaks down if the spouses have no caring time for one another. The same holds true for a priest's marriage to the Lord. Celibacy is not some kind of penitential burden that priests are asked to tolerate as a price to pay for their priesthood. The magnificence of celibacy is that it is a gifted and privileged presence I live, which hopefully opens me and affords me time to be with the Master. Surely, I can find the Lord in my people and in my caring, day-to-day ministry for them. My celibacy frees me for this active involvement. But if I am not able to discover the presence of the Lord in myself, then I am living in a fool's paradise, and the precious something that will have atrophied in me is the intimate experience of the Lord's presence. Parish priests spend endless hours debating this need

13. William Shakespeare, *The Complete Works of Shakespeare* (New York, NY: Halcyon House, 1960), V, v, 24-25.
14. Ibid., V, v, 27-28.

in their own lives. They insist that they are not monks or
religious per se. The difficulty that seems to be so often over-
looked, nevertheless, is the inconsistency of men who, although
they claim that the Lord lives in others, are not open to that
same living presence in themselves.

I certainly do not pretend to know how each particular priest
begins to make this time available for caring intimacy with the
Lord. Each priest has to make this prudent judgment himself.
He has to look at his own disposition, his daily responsibilities,
and many other factors that might be peculiar or unique to a
given parish setting. He has to listen to the rhythm of his daily
life in an obedient way. I use the term obedient, as van Kaam
does, because it comes from the two Latin words *ob* and *audire,*
which mean "to listen to." In listening to the situation of his
daily life, each priest has to begin to plan definite times in which
he can set himself apart for prayerful communion with the Lord.
Some priests might be able to do so early in the morning; others
might find the afternoon or evening hours more available for
such a practice. The parish is certainly far removed from the
disciplined structure of seminary formation. This is no excuse,
however, for not appropriating the value of a disciplined time
for prayer that is more in tune with parish life.

When I make time for prayer, which is apart from my
presence to my people, I have to face the question of whether I
can face myself in my aloneness. Can I be still? Can I be silent?
Do I enjoy the safe and secure ways of my taken-for-granted
presence with others? Is my level of immanence so strong that I
am threatened by the risk of turning my life around at a deeper
level and, in transcendent openness, returning to my Father's
house? Am I able to accept that I do not know, I do not see, I do
not have all the answers to life's mystery? Am I poor enough to
be my ordinary self, to be weak, to be vulnerable, to be broken?
Can I be poor enough to begin to experience myself as a child
who must entrust his life to a Father who alone ultimately knows

and sees my original call? Can I dare to risk letting the Lord enter into my life and care for me, not as the perfect one, but as the sinner, the one filled with imperfections, shortcomings, and failures? Can I face the question that is still asked of all men, "Adam, where are you?"[15] Can I admit as Adam admitted, "I was afraid because I was naked, so I hid" (Gen. 3:20)? Can I accept that, as a priest, my life can become filled with illusory hideouts from naked presence with the Lord? Can I admit that I too have often been the hireling who has no real concern for the sheep but probably more concern for the immanent dimension of preserving my own self-centered place? Can I let myself be sinner and, from that fundamental realization, become open to the healing presence of my Father who has sent his Son into the world to call me back as his adopted child?

When I reflect in this fashion and ask these kind of questions of myself, I think of how my development in prayer has been quite the opposite. As a seminarian, I was always striving for perfection and covering up my imperfection. I tried to live the illusion that God only likes perfect people and that, to be a good priest, I must become a perfect saint. I forgot that Christ entered the world because God loved sinners. In fact, the Christ of the Gospels is one who walked and ate constantly with sinners. His closest friends, such as the apostles, were ordinary men who were filled with imperfections and shortcomings. The first Pope, the rock on which Christ built his Church, crumbled to pieces in denying his Lord. Finally, Peter, like all Christians, came to realize that the true rock was Christ. On the rock of Christ's presence in his life and not on his own self, Peter built the early foundations of the Church.

Going apart from the busy world to find time for the stillness of prayer was interestingly captured by Father Hugh Kennedy in

---

15. Refer to *Personal Care and Pastoral Presence,* pp. 212-14. Here I discuss the Genesis account of God's question to Adam as asked universally of all men.

The Edge of Sadness when he found himself in the Arizona desert at a residence called the Cenacle. During his attempt to put his life back together again he observed:

> Often, driving back to the Cenacle at night, I found that I could think about things I hadn't really thought about for years. . . . passing through the strange quiet and the clear shining darkness of the desert night, I would suddenly become aware of a stillness which was something quite apart from the stillness of the night. It was an interior stillness, a stillness inside me, a stillness in which there was the absence of all distraction and unrest, a stillness in which, quietly and without effort, I seemed to come together, to be focused and attentive, to be really present, so to speak, a stillness from which it seemed natural, even inevitable, to reach out, to pray, to adore . . . at last I came to terms with myself and with God.[16]

Now the average priest does not have to have a breakdown or suffer from alcoholism to realize that finding time to go apart and be still is important. The original Cenacle was a place of prayer in the early Christian community. It was here that the Apostles and the early disciples waited in prayer for the gift of Pentecost. In each priest's life there must be a personal time and place for prayer, a personal cenacle, a personal desert moment in which daily the parish priest becomes aware of an interior stillness, an ability to come together and be really present not only to himself but to the Lord. In this light, it might be fruitful for parish priests to wonder about the present phenomenon of so many people flocking to transcendental gurus in search of spiritual stillness. We can cynically scoff at such "nonsense." However, the "nonsense" of the matter might possibly be a sign that, as parish priests, we have not witnessed to a deep spiritual life that people hunger for in today's society. How do our people see us? Are we stuck in the taken-for-granted immanence of everyday life, or are we living signs of openness to the transcendent? Such transcendent openness is tested and matures

---

16. O'Connor, pp. 155-56.

in the time I care to provide for a day-to-day going apart to be with the Lord through the mystery of prayer.

TIME TO BE PRESENT WITH PEOPLE[17]

The more I find time to let the Lord come into my life and care for me, the more I let the priests and people I live with nurture me with their care, the easier it becomes to be comfortable with myself. It is only from this basic self-comfort that I can genuinely offer care to the people who enter my life.[18] I find that I am no longer giving one person five minutes here, another person a half an hour there. My life is no longer fragmented and measured in intervals of time. Instead, my life is me. My life becomes my presence to myself in a centered way. It is the difference between experiencing myself moving patiently from a centrifugal "scattering" to a centripetal balance and integration. Around myself as comfortable, self-esteeming center and resting within the horizon of God's care, I now begin to discover and establish basic priorities and a genuine hierarchy of values that are congenial to or in tune with my fundamental uniqueness and originality. I am no longer a threatened possession that I have to hold on to in my relationships with others. Instead, I am a precious gift that God has chosen to share with others.

When I am with another person in counseling, talking on the telephone, or whatever, I am there as a personal presence to the personal presence of the other. I am "I," and the other is "Thou." When I am listening to the other, I am not projecting myself into planning or worrying about what I have to do an

---

17. Refer to *Personal Care and Pastoral Presence,* pp. 31-33, in which I discuss Martin Heidegger's consideration of existential time. Refer also to pp. 174-77, in which I discuss Martin Buber's understanding of dialogical presence.

18. Refer to the appendix of *Personal Care and Pastoral Presence,* pp. 641-52. Rev. Alfred Hughes, spiritual director of Saint John's Seminary, Boston, MA, uses the term "self-comfort" as a sign of mature growth in evaluating the life of a seminarian.

hour from now. I am not concerned with what happened to me an hour ago. To the contrary, I am able to be completely there in the present with another person. Being present, in the present time we now share, is my gift of presence. When my care gets stuck in the past or runs ahead into the future, I live with a care that becomes heavy, agitated, and uncomfortable. Only when I free myself to be my real self here and now, to care for the issue of what is happening between me and the other as he or she really is now, only then is care genuine presence.

What I am suggesting here is not a foreign experience in the lives of parish priests or, for that matter, in the lives of most people. There are countless occasions when I can be with another person and not really be there. I can be eyeball to eyeball with the other, know just when to nod my head or say yes or no, and yet my real self can be a million miles away. I am merely putting in time or maybe even killing time. When I no longer have to hold on to my immanent self in order to be safe and secure, when I no longer have to manage and control life, then the time and care I live is an open offering to my world. My care becomes transcendent. It is open because I am open. The day I live is no longer "my" day but the Lord's day. This state-ment might sound pious, but it is a profound truth. My day-to-day existence is fundamentally not mine. It is a gift entrusted to me freely and generously by God himself. All my anxious worry over time for this and time for that is my usurpation of God's sovereign power over the gift of day-to-day life. When I am with another person, that relationship is a gifted moment, for ultimately this meeting together also rests in the providential plan of God. When I make this gifted moment into "my" mo-ment, then I isolate myself from the ultimate horizon in which all life rests.

How many times do I catch myself worrying about what tomorrow is going to bring in my life? Let us say I have an im-portant talk to give to a large gathering of people. Do I begin to worry about how I will be received? Am I really prepared? Will I say the right thing? My care for tomorrow becomes heavy and uncomfortable. Time drags as I anticipate what will happen. In fact, I may even "kill" the present in order to distract myself from worrying over the future. My attempt is to reach into tomorrow and make it all mine. My care for tomorrow becomes grabby, forced, and anxious. Meanwhile, I miss the beauty of living fully what I am doing today. I miss the realization and acceptance that tomorrow is not mine. It is the Lord's day. It is the Lord's gift. The same holds true for being with another troubled person. I can become anxious about whether I am really helping, whether I care enough. I lose sight of the fact that what is happening right now between me and the other is God's gift. Too many priests, who claim that they have given their lives over to the Lord, show in their everyday experience that they have more confidence in their own clever ways than they have genuine living trust in the gracious giftedness of God's presence living moment-to-moment in daily life. Again, the immanent dimension of making sure, being safe, knowing what to do, becomes the texture of such care. Life becomes a never-ending series of problems in which I spend all of my time concerned about trying to keep everything going, everything fitting together according to my blueprint. I experience the immanent dimension of time and close myself off from the liberating freedom of being open to the transcendent horizon in which all life ultimately rests.

RECTORY SPACE[19]

As a parish priest, I have always noticed that I enjoy going home to my parents' house and also visiting the homes of friends because there is space to relax and be myself. One of the terrible

---

19. Refer to *Personal Care and Pastoral Presence,* pp. 28-29, in which I discuss Martin Heidegger's consideration of existential spatiality. Refer also to pp. 30-31, footnote #7, for excellent resource material on the dimensions of human spatiality.

dilemmas of rectory living in most priests' lives is that rectories, for the most part, can often be just houses and not really homes. The great difficulty here is the fact that the parish house is too often just a place of work. Priests have not taken the time or the care to make their house a home. As priests, we have allowed ourselves no genuine living space in which to relax and be ourselves. The more a priest can begin to let go of his feverish need to be constantly busy, the more he might take a second look at the space in which he lives.

A rectory should have work space, living together space, and private space. In many rectories these three separate spaces get mixed together. With regard to work space, I think priests have to be more aware of what a cold and lifeless room means, not only to themselves, but to the many people who visit this room. In many rectories one can find cramped little rooms in which Father is expected to carry on his "business" with parishioners. Such rooms are usually filled with a big desk that takes up most of the space. Father is expected to sit behind the desk and fill out forms, whereas parishioners are left to sit on old rickety chairs that should have been sold as antiques many years ago. Some "modern" priests have felt that folding steel chairs are the best way to save space in cramped offices. The problem with meeting people in rooms that are merely functionally oriented is that usually people cannot feel at home. I cannot ever imagine Christ sitting behind a desk and meeting people in some of the rooms that we call offices. No human being in his right mind can ever feel at home in such a milieu. The magnificence of Christ's care was that people were able to feel at home in his presence. If feeling at home was the mystery of Christ's caring presence, I have to think seriously about how I offer rectory space as a sign of hospitable care.

Is it so out of the question to spend a few extra dollars in rethinking the space of my rectory? Do we really need all the desks that clutter up much of our space? Are they not rather a sign of keeping a safe distance from our people? And what about those chairs? Is it too much to ask that we might consider appointing our rooms with comfortable easy chairs in which people can begin to sit down and feel at home? Can we afford not to buy a rug that gives a sense of warmth? Are the pictures that hang on our walls the leftover relics of some old rectory attic? Does the poor parishioner have to sit in a room where the picture of the Archbishop glowers down on him? Is it really out of the question to ask some of the women in the parish to take a look at our rectory space and offer suggestions about how to make our "offices" into a more gracious home? Might I offer coffee or a refreshing cold drink to people who come to visit? These are just a few of the many questions that a parish priest could profit from in re-evaluating the rectory space in which he lives and cares for his people. We can never lose sight of the fact that people want to feel at home in the presence of their priests, and, I hope, the same holds true for priests who should want to be at home with their people.

Living together space for the priests of a rectory is very important. In some big rectories, each priest may have a bedroom and an adjoining study. One of the sad commentaries on rectory living can be that each priest disappears into his own little cubicle and lives by himself because there is not a comfortable room in which the priests can relax and be together. The homes of most people will always have some kind of living room space in which the whole family can gather and share with one another. The same should hold true for the common living room of the rectory. Priests should be encouraged to be with one another in such living space. Such a room should not be the private preserve and responsibility of the pastor. If rectory living is to become a more caring community, then each of the men who lives in the house should be able to share in the appointing and planning of such space. Too many curates have retreated to the privacy of their own rooms because the common room has been the possession of the pastor. Curates should not have to live in the pastor's house; a community of priests should be able to live comfortably together in "their" home. A closer reflection on this simple, taken-for-granted matter of rectory space can tell us a great deal about our fundamental concerns in life and how we really feel about ourselves and one another.[20] It would be interesting to know how many priests ever examine their consciences concerning how they make living room or living space for one another in day-to-day rectory living. Most priests never do so, which is again a concrete sign of how easily we can be locked into an immanent way of life and not realize how closed we are to one another as real persons.

Private space is also a necessity in rectory life. A priest should have a room that is large enough to provide him a study. The active priest has to find a space apart from the whirlwind of activities. He should be able to appoint this space in a way that suits his temperament and taste. Again, he should be able to feel at home in his room. He should feel free, once he moves into a new parish as a replacement for a former priest who has been transfered, to redecorate the room according to his wishes and not have to live with the taste of the man who preceded him. This room is his room and not the pastor's room. The old idea that curates serve at the behest of the pastor and live in "his house" is antiquated and ridiculous. As a curate I am not a boarder in somebody else's house where the somebody else is master and I am servant. A house full of priests is full of masters in the Christian sense, men who are so because they are servants to one another. Not only should I be provided with decent and suitable living quarters that I can experience as my own private space, but my fellow priests should allow me to have the recreative privacy I need to be alone, to reflect, to pray, to study, and to draw apart in order to return to active engagement.

When I draw apart from my fellow priests and go to my room,

20. Robert Sommer, *Tight Spaces* (New York, NY: Prentice-Hall, Inc., 1974).

my action is not an open invitation for somebody else in the house to visit me and interrupt me constantly. Thus a separate living together space such as a common room is important in rectory living. A common room allows me to have my own separate space in my own study. This rhythm of being together and also preserving our separateness is critical in rectory living. It is up to the priests of each rectory to establish a rhythm that is in tune with their various dispositions and responsibilities. One priest might require more solitude and privacy than another. Another priest might need to be together with his associates more than another. The important feature of gracious living space, whether it be space we share in common or space we enjoy privately, is that priests are obedient and respectful of themselves as well as of one another. The obedient man, to use van Kaam's thoughts, is the man who listens (*ob-audire*) to the day-to-day situation of his life with others. He is the man who sees deeper (*re-spicere*) than the surface taken-for-granted patterns. He hears and sees what is truly going on in his own life and is open to hearing and seeing what is going on in the lives of his priest associates. Such a priest, who is sensitively tuned into his own real needs as a person and the real needs of his associates, is able to let himself be himself and let others be themselves. I let the other have the space he needs to be the person he is at the present moment, and, I hope, he gives me the same space to be myself.

An answering service, which most communities provide for people who are always on call, enables a priest to find more time and space for himself. Doctors, funeral directors, and many other professionals and business people use such a service today. Many priests think that such a device is too impersonal and that parishioners will not appreciate it. I seriously wonder if this belief is as true as it might first appear. People can appreciate that the priests of their parish must have some time and space for themselves. If the people are told why some of their calls to the rectory will be answered by an answering service, they will understand. Emergency calls still can be handled quickly. An answering service allows a priest to live a normal life free from nuisance calls that can be handled expeditiously without constantly interfering with the time and space that a priest could be using for higher priorities. There is no need for a priest to have to sit on "duty" in a rectory waiting for people to have emergencies or come to visit. An answering service gives a priest the flexibility to get out of the rectory to be with people where they are really living their lives. It provides him with time and space to relax away from and in the rectory.

THE LEISURELY MAN[21]

In the Church today there is great distress about the lack of candidates to the priesthood and religious life. Many priests wonder what is wrong. Why does not the life of a parish priest interest young men? I would suggest that young people want to live and enjoy life. They have been brought up in a postwar time in which this country has provided them with "the good life." I have a suspicion that these same young people are not attracted to the modern image of the priesthood basically because they have experienced too many priests who appear not to enjoy the calling they are living. The priesthood of recent times has gone through an agonizing reappraisal, as has our whole society. The result has too often been a characterization that might be described as a priest wearing a worried look and carrying the weight of the world on his shoulders. In a sense, we might possibly have taken ourselves too seriously. We appear to be overburdened with work and all "scrunched up" with the heavy cares and worries of our world. Many of us have lived Saint Paul's words in reverse order:

---

21. Refer to *Personal Care and Pastoral Presence,* pp. 112-13. Here I discuss Josef Pieper's understanding of the leisurely attitude.

> Because we possess this ministry of ourselves, we do give into
> discouragement. It is ourselves we preach and not Christ Jesus
> as Lord. . . . This treasure we possess in perfect vessels to
> make it clear that its surpassing power comes from ourselves
> and not from God. We are afflicted in every way and we
> despair. Continually, we carry about in our bodies the dying of
> Jesus in order to be pitied by men. We are constantly being
> delivered to suffering for our own sake, so that our lives may
> be revealed . . . we cannot sympathize with those who are ig-
> norant or uncertain because we live too often in the illusion of
> perfection.[22]

Such an image of the priest certainly is not inviting and certainly exhibits a lack of trust and hope in the presence of the
Lord. Unfortunately, I am afraid that this "bad news" syn-
drome is what has happened to many priests. They have put
themselves so much in charge of the Lord's affairs that there
really is not much room left to discover the presence of the Lord.
John the Baptist understood this dilemma better than anyone
else. He knew that his ministry was a pointing to the Lord. In the
lives of his disciples, he knew that he had to decrease while the
Lord must increase. John was a man who was open to the meaning of who he really was. He did not get stuck in the immanence
of resting with the acclaim and approval of his followers. The
transcendent dimension of his life was a humble and trusting
openness that led people to the Lord.

I suspect that John was able to be a witness to the Lord
because he was a leisurely man. He understood his unique and
original call and, from this fundamental rooting in his real self,
he was strong enough to be open to the advent of the Lord as the
ultimate and saving ground of all life. This man had spent practically his entire life in the desert preparing himself for the coming of the Messiah. His desert experience was a waste of time in
the eyes of many of his contemporaries. To disengage himself
from the everyday life of Jewish society and enter into deep

---

22. This quotation is a negative rephrasing of Saint Paul's Epistles, 2
Corinthians and Hebrews.

reflection about who he was and what he was called to proclaim was thought to be nonsense and madness. Life in the desert was a totally useless affair in the minds of the common people. However, we know that the impact that this man had on the people was tremendous when he came to preach not himself but the advent of the Lord.

And so it must be with ourselves as priests. The leisurely attitude is not the idle attitude. Idleness is the refusal to be what I fundamentally am, a despairing refusal to be myself. Idleness renders leisure impossible. Leisure, on the other hand, is an acquiescence in my own being in which I am one with myself. It is an attitude of nonactivity, of inward calm, of silence. It means not being busy but letting life happen. When I am leisurely, I do not have to grab hold of life and try to possess it. I am able to let the reins loose and be free and easy with myself. Leisure is a receptive or open attitude in which I can steep myself in the meaning of my own wholeness and the wholeness of life. As a leisurely person, I become centered in myself as one who has come home to the deep presence and power of the Lord living within me.

The leisurely priest realizes that he does not possess this ministry of himself and thus does not have to be discouraged. The ministry he shares is ultimately the Lord's. The leisurely priest realizes that he is an earthen vessel and that it is okay to be imperfect, for the surpassing power of his ministry comes not from himself but from God. He can deliver himself over to suffering and carrying the death of Christ in his own life, for the leisurely priest is an Easter person who believes in the miracle of new life. He can sympathize with those who are ignorant or uncertain because he is not the perfect one but one who, like his brothers and sisters, lives with the limitations of his own human weakness.

When I am leisurely as a priest, I can accept that I am an ordinary person. I do not have to have extraordinary expectations for myself and for others. I can wear a smile and be happy with being an ordinary person. The whole future of the Church and the world does not rest on my shoulders, but again it is the Lord's Church and the Lord's world. I do not have to take my life so seriously that I forget that the world has been entrusted to Christ by his Father. I have Christ's assurance that no one can steal from his Father. It is not my light that shines in the darkness of the day-to-day world. As a leisurely man, I begin to realize more and more that the Light is Christ's life. I have his assurance that the darkness can never overpower the Light. I am called to share in his Light, not in my own light. That is the ultimate meaning of my life as servant of the children of God.

As a leisurely person, I can be an okay person. For young people it is this model of Christian ministry that begins to make sense. No matter what happens to me in my day-to-day life, I am able to remain peacefully and gracefully together. I do not have to come apart at the seams and proclaim doom and bad news. I experience a wholeness to my life that rests in the meaningful wholeness of God's providential care for his world. I can be relaxed rather than uptight in my associations with others. I can have time and patience with people who need understanding. I offer hope rather than condemnation and criticism. I can "waste time" on myself and "waste time" merely being with people in a friendly way, without having to consider some extraordinary cause or great difficulty to make our being together meaningful. The very fact that I am who I am is the most important event in my life. God has loved me into existence, and, consequently, I can find time and space to be comfortably present with the precious gift of my own existence.

In the presence of a leisurely priest, people begin to feel that it is okay to relax and be comfortable because Father shares with them the gift of his original self. He does not have to play roles and pretend to be perfect. He can be truly "parochial" or *para-oikein* in the sense of "living near by" his people, and he can experience the ordinary rhythm of life as the opening to God's tenting place among man.

When I am leisurely, I can actually walk through the forest and see and hear aspects of life I have never experienced before because I no longer have to hold on. I am receptively open. The forest begins to speak new meanings to me. The same holds true in living with people in a parish. When I become more leisurely in my approach to parishioners, I begin to hear and see a magnificent goodness and secret beauty that I was often too busy to experience in the past. People no longer have to be problems and interruptions in my life. Each person I meet becomes a living sacrament of God's presence, blessing me and helping me to grow and emerge as a deeper self. People are no longer threatened by being in my presence because, in my leisurely openness, they begin to experience a deeper and more authentic presence of God's goodness and care for them. The leisurely man grows with the understanding that in some mysterious way his deepest self is the self of all men, and it is the shared meaning and the shared caring for who I really am and who the other really is that makes all the difference in the world, not only for me but for the flock that is entrusted to me.

As a leisurely person, I can find time and space to recreate. I understand that recreational pauses are important conditions for re-creating my oftentimes tired spirit. I can enjoy leaving my work and turning to a good novel or a walk through town or into the country. I can find the opportunity to telephone someone to stay in touch or to write a personal letter. I can understand the importance of taking vacation time and regular days off in order to get away from a world that can truly get along without me. My play does not have to be "worked at" but is freely enjoyed at a relaxed pace. As a priest, I have the gift of celibate free time to take advantage of opportunities to spend a day in prayerful recollection or to experience a week's spiritual retreat to deepen my intimate growth in the Lord. I begin to appreciate that a leisurely pace enables me to be myself and to be one who is comfortable enough to care more authentically for the people I serve.

THE PLAYFUL MAN[23]

A leisurely person is an interesting and enjoyable person, for he is able to be playful. Leisure and play go together. Human beings need to play. Playfulness is in the very nature of man. It is the spontaneous expression of the fact that one enjoys a situation when there is absence of weighty concern and worry. To be real, play must be free, born from within, and not imposed on me from without. When play is considered as a possibility for parish priests, many people immediately think that such activity means playing with young people or becoming a glorified coach or cheerleader for the athletic achievements of young parishioners. Such play, of course, is not the kind to which I refer. Many young priests feel that play, understood in the context of the Bing Crosby "Going My Way" image, is something that they have to avoid at all costs. Consequently, many priests have overcompensated for this refusal to play; they take care of the youths of their parishes by becoming professionally involved in much more serious causes. They have possibly taken themselves too seriously and have forgotten that even Christ was not too busy to find time for the children he placed in his own lap and played with.

When I suggest play as an important quality for a caring priest, I mean that a priest should be able to let himself enjoy life. A priest's call is the call to be a celebrating man, which is the highest form of leisurely and meaningful play. It has always been a disappointment to me that I have never seen a painting or picture of a smiling Christ. Even in the Gospels there is no account of Christ laughing or smiling. Somehow this is a tragedy,

---

23. Refer to *Personal Care and Pastoral Presence,* pp. 113-15, in which I discuss Remy C. Kwant's consideration of the playful attitude.

for I am sure that Christ did smile. A Perfect Man could not help laughing and smiling many times in his lifetime, for a Perfect Man would necessarily be a celebrating man. Christ came as the Logos, as one affirming the ultimate meaning of the universe. He was the joyful one who constantly gave praise to the glory of the Father by being completely and fully in tune with the rhythm of his everyday life. I am sure that he even laughed and smiled at the serious pretensions of his disciples.

I am playful or a celebrating priest when I lose my wrinkled and worried look and begin to realize that life can be lived with a smile and deep joy. Recently a new Pope was chosen. Time and again we have seen that this man, John Paul I, is able to laugh at himself and smile. We like him because he seems so real. I too can be happy and enjoy my life if I live with the realization that life and death are not opponents but do, in fact, kiss each other at every moment of existence.[24] Life leads to death, and death opens to the transcendence of new life. When I am born, I become free to breathe on my own, but I lose the safety of my mother's womb. When I go to school, I am free to join a greater society but lose a particular cozy and secure place in my home. When I marry, I find a new partner but lose the special tie I had with my parents. When I find work, I win more independence but lose the stimulation of teachers and fellow students. When I receive children into my family, I discover a new world but lose much of my old freedom to move. When I am promoted, I become more important in the eyes of others but lose the chance to take as many new risks. When I retire, I finally have the chance to do what I want but lose the support of being wanted. Life is a gaining and a losing. Life and death touch each other constantly, and I am able to celebrate this everyday rhythm because I realize that the man who loses his life can find it. It is

---

24. Henri J. M. Nouwen, *Creative Ministry* (Garden City, NY: Doubleday & Co., 1971), pp. 89-108. This book treats the mystery of the celebrating priest in an extensive way.

this fundamental irony in the mystery of life that is the root of my celebration.

The celebrating man understands that immanence is not the final answer. The celebrating and playful person is one who experiences a sense of distance. In such a reflective pause and recollected dwelling, his spirit is always open to the transcedent miracle of new life. He does not merely react to life but responds. He is in tune with the fundamental mystery of life's constant unfolding against the ultimate horizon of God's providential presence. The celebrating priest certainly is not one who is crushed; nor does he live in despair. His playful attitude is always open. He is the prophet who celebrates not only the present but calls his people forth to the possibilities of their future. He trusts that the Kingdom of God is present and offers the vision of a life-giving hope that witnesses to the joy of being an Easter person.

Translated into the ministry of the parish priest, this definition means that I am able to celebrate the liturgy as the prayerful playground that expresses the Easter meaning of life triumphing over death. The daily liturgy is no longer a duty, a burden, a job to be done. It is a celebrating and playfully free community gathering together in order to express its thanksgiving and joy about the mystery of new life triumphing over death. The liturgy becomes a sacred play in which I become open to remembering my roots in tradition and recognizing and making visibly present the presence of the risen Lord. A child stands in the castle of his sand box and playfully proclaims himself as king. As priest, I stand in the situation of everyday life, in the sacred space of the church, and in the sacred festival time of the liturgical celebration. I sacramentally proclaim the good news that the Lord is King. He is risen, and anyone who lives and believes in the Lord will never die. Each day I stand at the altar of the Lord, I call my people present there to his Easter presence. We are one family and, one hopes, the world can look at us and see that we truly

love and care for one another, that we enjoy walking in the
footsteps of the Lord, that we enjoy the companionship of
journeying to Emmaus in his presence. New life is present in our
lives. In celebration we affirm or make this life visible so that we
can say yes to it.

In playful celebration of baptism, the daily Eucharist, marriage, penance, holy anointing, or a funeral liturgy, I am able to
be free enough to be myself. I am free to speak out of my real experience in life. I do not have to be heavy or cerebral; I can be
light and honestly genuine. At life-affirming moments when the
sacraments are celebrated, people are not spiritually fed and
uplifted by safe and lifeless tracts in theology. To the contrary,
as parish priest, I have to be able to take my theological
background and become open to how this theology speaks in living experience in my own life and in the lives of my people. I
must learn to play with the symbols and common experiences of
men to draw out new life.[25] To do so, I must let go of an immanent fixation with a mere theologizing that is safe and so often
lifeless because it can stand at a distance and speculate and talk
"about life." Christ was not first and foremost a theologian or a
moralist. He came proclaiming himself as the Way, the Truth,
and the Life. He was free enough to play openly with everyday
life. He could talk about seeds, fishing nets, bread, water,
shepherds, sheep, wedding feasts, and many other common,
ordinary persons, events, and things in daily life and draw forth
living lessons. He did not talk "about life" from a safe distance
but offered the life he experienced day to day as spiritual food.
Ultimately, he offered his own life.

Is it not interesting that when I stand in a pulpit and preach *at*
people and offer them all kinds of profound insights *about* life
and God, they do not listen? The second I am able to be free
enough to translate what I am talking about into a living

---

25. Refer to *Personal Care and Pastoral Presence,* pp. 559-61. Here I
discuss Adrian van Kaam's consideration of man's preconscious level of
presence as the source of creative free association.

witness, my own witness or the witness of another person, people come alive and listen. In other words, as human beings we thrive on life that is shared, not on life that is talked about and that generates so much hot air in the windmills of the mind. In this vein, why is it that most people enjoy children? I think the answer is that a child is not usually afraid of being himself. He or she is usually openly free and spontaneous, filled with countless questions, surprises, and new life. A child can easily melt the coldest heart. Is it any wonder, then, that Christ reminded us that unless we become as little children we would not enter into the Kingdom of God? We priests share the life-giving kingdom with our people when we dare to risk letting our child-like self emerge. Being a strong and blustery adult is one of the easiest ways to turn people off. There is no warmth and tenderness in a person who cannot be childlike. We can easily warm up to those persons who do not need to defend or cover up the precious goodness of who they are.

More of us as priests could profit by spending time observing and even playing with children. We do not have children of our own, and we tend to forget what childhood is all about. We even pretend that we do not have to be childlike, for it is unbecoming in an adult. The last thing I ever want to hear about myself is that I am considered to be "naive." To be naive is thought to be imperfect, to be stupid, to be no more than a simple child, and of no account. In living with children and observing their playful nature, however, a priest might grow more present to his own goodness and realize that the naive world of children has profound lessons to teach. Maybe a priest could learn that a child's play is never a job, never a worrisome burden. Play is completely free and open. A child does not have to have great objectives and is hardly ever tense. In a child's play, there is an exuberance and spontaneity, an enjoyment of life that makes life worth living. Would it not be interesting if some of these playful attitudes could rub off on our ministry of caring for others in the celebrating mood of liturgical worship and interpersonal relationships? Would it not be wonderful to experience young people as well as older people observing the lives of priests and saying to themselves: yes, here is a vocation that is very relevant in a gloomy world because the lives of these men bespeak the *joie de vivre* of Easter resurrection seven days a week? To those who worry about vocation shortages, I would humbly suggest that all the current Madison Avenue approaches amount to nothing compared to the attractive living presence of a parish priest whose daily life witnesses to the "good news" conviction that priesthood is very much alive and well.

THE WONDERING MAN[26]

The parish priest is called to be a living witness of God's presence in daily life. However, if I am incapable of finding time and space to pause and reflect over the question I am and the questions life poses, then I become lost in the immanence of being merely a hollow man. One of the great gifts that the priest enjoys as a privilege is the state of celibacy. Celibacy is given to me by God as an opportunity to be open to wondering over the mystery of life. As a priest, I am "set apart" and called to dwell upon the mystery of daily realities. The average parishioner is usually too busy to spend time in deep reflection. He or she has the immediate responsibility of a spouse and family and the constant care of providing a decent livelihood for them. I am freed of family responsibility and the constant care which goes with it in order that I might care for discovering the deeper horizon and value of life. Of course, I am not suggesting that a married person cannot be a wondering person or one dedicated to discovering deep value. I am suggesting, however, that my whole life is a call to be a radical value center that discovers, reveals, and radiates essential and ultimate values to my wider culture.

---

26. Refer to *Personal Care and Pastoral Presence,* pp. 118-21, in which I discuss Bernard J. Boelen's consideration of the wondering attitude.

Adrian van Kaam understands the meaning of religious life and community from the perspective of offering religious value to the wider culture[27] He points out that it is tremendously important to have value centers that preserve and radiate their influence throughout the culture, especially when certain values are threatened or repressed. In today's modern society, which has repressed the transcendent religious dimension of life, it is even more important that radiating centers of religious value continue to exist. The parish priest cooperates in the value center of the bishop of his diocese. He is the radiating spoke or extension of the bishop's pastoral presence at the parish level. My day-to-day presence is the call to witness to values that often will not be applauded or approved because such values have slipped out of the conscious and explicit life patterns of so many people. The immanent dimension has become the way for so many. Most people want to be safe and secure in today's world. Such social issues as equal and low-cost housing, governmental and educational integrity and responsibility, concern for the spiritual welfare of the affluent as well as the poor, and many others are often the modern stations of the cross at which a parish priest is called to witness to ultimate Christian values. The parish priest may become the transcendent "disturber" in many people's lives if growth and maturity are to win out over conformity, mediocrity, and spiritual blindness.

If I do not give myself the space and time to dwell and recollect, I cannot be a value center for my people; I cannot point to God's mysterious presence in the persons, events, and things of daily life. Many people living functionally ordered lives are ready to give instructions on "how" life should be led. As the wondering one, I am called to ask the question "why," to search for and be open to answers that possibly lead to deeper

---

27. Adrian van Kaam, *The Vowed Life* (Denville, NJ: Dimension Books, 1968), pp. 41-51. The author discusses the importance of centers of value radiation.

questions because I am living, ultimately, within the horizon of the unfathomable mystery of God's presence. I cannot force the mystery of life to speak to me. I cannot force answers to complex issues and lose a balanced sense of prudence. I can only place myself in humble readiness to listen and see when life chooses to bless me with its gifted meanings. I have to ask myself whether my life style is one of calculating or meditative presence.[28] The calculating person is always planning, computing, analyzing, and racing from one prospect to another. He never stops and never collects himself. A calculating person can enjoy the spectacular and likes to look good in the eyes of his contemporaries or in the eyes of some small group in which he has invested his crusading energies. He expects results and is willfully oriented. The meditative thinker, on the contrary, is able to stop and rest. He is able to wait for meaning and for the proper time to say and do the right thing. He is the faithful disciple, one who follows the offered meanings of life rather than one who forcefully projects meaning onto life. Such a wondering man does not need to be agitated, impatient, or impetuous. He is in tune with the deeper harmony of life as orchestrated and directed by God. Such a man can be responsibly strong, comfortably relaxed, and involved with life's complexity in a wise way because he is not rooted in the pride system of reactive ideals or vital needs but deeply anchored in God's unfolding mystery and providence.[29] His spirit life gives him the energy to pause and wonderingly reflect on the deeper meaning of past, present, and future reality.

The leisurely, playful, wondering attitude also has a tremendous importance for any priest who wants to care deeply for a life of prayer, meditative reading, and growth in spiritual in-

28. Refer to *Personal Care and Pastoral Presence,* p. 122, footnote #50. Here I discuss Martin Heidegger's understanding of the difference between calculating and meditative thinking.
29. Refer to *Personal Care and Pastoral Presence,* pp. 8-16, wherein I discuss Adrian van Kaam's spiritual personality theory.

timacy with the presence of the Lord. In my thesis, I discuss in detail the conditions that foster such a transcendent openness.[30] Here, however, I want to suggest that people may fall asleep during our Sunday sermons because we have nothing to say. Maybe we are repeating old theological axioms that people have heard a million times before and that no longer carry life or speak to modern experience. A man like Henry David Thoreau went into the woods to steep himself in the experience of wondering over the mystery of life.[31] He went into the woods, however, in order that he might return to daily life a more deeply enriched person. He was not an escapist. So it must be with the parish priest who wants to feed his flock at a deeper level of life. During a day I have to find time and space to draw apart, to reflect and wonder about what is going on in my life and what is going on in the lives of my parishioners. How does parish life relate to the good news of the Gospel? What is really going on in our lives and why?

It is interesting to observe that doctors, lawyers, counselors, and many other people in the helping professions take notes during their interviews with people and that yet, for the most part, priests do not do so. Priests may confidently feel that they can "fly by the seat of their pants" and know at all times what is going on in life without reflective preparation or reflective afterthought. The tragedy of such a cozy and secure immanence is that these priests can be closed to the deeper mystery that is always present in the ordinary day-to-day rhythms. I am suggesting, therefore, that a priest could gain a great deal for himself and for his parishioners if, after meeting with people or following any event during his day, he scribbled down a few pertinent notes on what happened. On a later occasion these notes

---

30. Refer to pp. 571-74, in which I discuss Adrian van Kaam's transcendent self-presence.
31. Refer to *Personal Care and Pastoral Presence,* pp. 91-95, in which I discuss Thoreau's spiritual retreat into the woods of Walden Pond.

could become a tremendous reservoir for recollecting his thoughts, his impressions, and his experiences and organizing them into an integrated whole. With such a practice, I can take the diffuse experience of God's presence at every moment of my life and experience that presence in a concentrated moment of deep reflection and open prayer.[32]

If someone were to ask what is the most important condition for developing a deeper spiritual life in the parish priesthood, I would consider the wondering or reflective pause as the highest priority. Life in a parish can be very much like the road to Emmaus. If I am not open to letting the presence of the Lord speak to me, I often may walk that road not knowing what I am doing and where I am going. Christ met the two disciples on the original road to Emmaus, and he called them "foolish men" because they were so slow to believe the full message of what went on in Jerusalem. If I am so busy that I cannot take the Jerusalem experience, the events, the persons, and the things that I meet each day into the recollected dwelling of a wondering pause, then I too am a foolish man. I can press the Lord to stay with me when "it is nearly evening and the day is almost over" only in prayerful reflection. I can go over the events of my day and in the presence of the Lord my eyes may be also opened to "all things that have been happening" in my life.

If the Lord himself over and over again in the Gospel accounts drew away from his activities and his disciples in order to be by himself and together with his Father, why is it that as parish priests we can so often think that such solitary moments are not necessary for us? We try to convince ourselves that our work is our prayer. In a beautiful and very real sense, we do so because it is in feeding the sheep that we indicate our love for the Lord according to the instructions given to Peter. This is the diffuse presence of the Lord living in the least of his brethren. However,

---

32. Refer to *Personal Care and Pastoral Presence,* pp. 598-622. Here I discuss the constructive use of a reflective and spiritual journal.

if I am incapable of meeting the Lord in concentrated moments of intimate reflection and quiet prayer, this diffuse presence of the Lord will eventually disappear, and my work will become just that, work. I will have lost the presence of personally experiencing the Lord walking with me.

A wondering person has to learn that being alone is not the greatest tragedy in life. I cannot wonder and reflect deeply upon the ultimate meaning of my life call if I always have to be with others. My celibate state gives me the opportunity to be alone and to care for the rich insights that creatively surface in the quiet and stillness of a temporary solitude. If I have noted what has gone on in my life on a particular day, my recollection in solitude does not have to be some kind of ivory tower escape from the real world. Rather, I can gather together the fragments of my daily experiences and ponder the concrete life I really live. I invite Christ to be here with me, to open my eyes, my ears, my mind, my heart, and my soul to the life I am really living. To a world that so often claims that active involvement is the only relevancy in which the true apostle "should" live, I would suggest that active involvement without prayerful reflection is a fool's paradise. The parish priest who lives in the stormy waters of daily life has to seek consistently a quiet and still harbor or risk shipwreck, not only for himself but for the others who travel with him. In the last analysis, the man who is active and at the same time reflects deeply on the meaning of his activity is the true spiritual disciple of the Lord. He is open to watching and waiting upon the fragmented events of his life, and, like the good shepherd, he is able to call these fragments by their real names and gather his flock around the presence of the Lord and not merely around himself.

THE GENTLE MAN[33]

The more a man wonders about himself and the mystery of

---

33. Refer to *Personal Care and Pastoral Presence,* pp. 124-30, in which I discuss Adrian van Kaam's understanding of the gentle attitude.

life, the more he is able to come to recognize his limitations and weaknesses. As a parish priest, I am like the rest of men. I am not called by Christ to come apart from the crowd because I am more perfect or superior than others. In fact, I may truthfully be more foolish and less wise than the rest of men, as Saint Paul so insightfully said. I am called apart from the rest of men in order to serve them because I too live in the limitations of weakness. The gentle attitude is the recognition and acceptance that I am not perfect. I am very fragile and vulnerable. When I am gentle, I am able to accept that I do not have to be perfect, that I do not have to know all things, that I do not have to be always right, that I do not always have to look good. My gentle attitude enables me to be strong enough to be weak, strong enough to be an ordinary person. I do not have to live with an ideal or perfect self that demands extraordinary ways in myself and in others.

When I am gentle as a parish priest, I can become a congenial presence with my people. They need not be afraid of or threatened by my presence. They begin to recognize that it is less important to me that they hear my voice than that, in the earthen vessel of my day-to-day presence, they are able to distinguish a deeper treasure, the presence and voice of the Lord. People can be at home with me, for in truth they begin to feel at home with the Lord who speaks through the transparency of my limitations.

The gentle presence of the parish priest becomes ever so important in the sacrament of penance. If I am a gentle person, then the penitent can feel at home and at ease with sharing his or her own vulnerable and fragile nature. One of the most difficult situations in my life is to want to talk to someone in order to unburden my soul and then not to find someone whom I believe is gentle enough to understand me in all my weakness. Many parishioners hesitate and even refuse to confess their sins and difficulties to their parish priests because they feel threatened by the model of perfection that is so unrealistically presented at times. The priest who thunders a self-righteous fist on the pulpit Sunday after Sunday is not the first person one wants to meet in a darkened confessional box or an open reconciliation room. He is not the one I will feel free to speak to when I am troubled.

As van Kaam points out, to be gentle with others I first of all must be gentle with myself. Many of us priests can forget this principle and try to convey a counterfeit or hollow kind of gentleness to our people. But people are not so easily fooled. People can sense when my gentleness is merely a mask or an ideal way that I attempt to live for others. Therefore, I can profit by an honest attention to my own attitude toward myself. Can I forgive myself for not being perfect, for not measuring up, for often failing in my responsibilities, for being human like the rest of men? How do I meet my limitations? Do I live with a chisel and violently try to cut away my shortcomings? Am I always trying to overanalyze myself and figure out a more perfect way to live my life? Am I constantly putting myself down or rigidly disciplining myself in an inflexible and exacting way? Have I willfully covered over my limitations and pushed myself beyond them? Are all my emotions and feelings flat and lifeless because I have repressed my real life in the world? Can I waste time, or is everything in my life perfectly organized down to the last detail? Questions like these are important for any priest to consider because they are the kind of questions that parishioners have about us and never ask.

During my lifetime, I have over and over again prayed the Lord's prayer: "Forgive us our trespasses as we forgive those who trespass against us." For the most part, it is not too difficult to forgive those who trespass against us. The number one problem that I usually have as a human being is coming to the point of being able to forgive myself. The person who does more trespassing against me is me. My prodigal nature gets the best of me and hurts me. I am not always faithful to my unique and original call. I do not live up to my expectations of perfection, and I become disappointed in myself. There are many ways in which I can trespass against myself. To be a gentle person I have to learn gradually that, in spite of all my trespasses, I am essentially good. I can hate the sin but love and forgive the sinner, who is me. Now these are just words unless I can recognize and accept that I am a sinner.[34] If I cannot forgive myself, how can I be open to God's forgiveness? My inability to forgive myself is usually a subtle form of pride. I will not allow weakness and imperfection to be an integral part of my life. I "should" be different. I am a closed heart, no longer open to the mercy of God who shares his forgiveness to the extent that I am open to sharing mercy with myself and others. There is a profound lesson for all priests in the insightful parable of Christ about the Pharisee and the publican who came to the temple to pray. The ordinary man, the publican, had the humility and strength to be weak, to recognize and accept who he really was: "Lord, forgive me, I am a sinner" (Luke 18:13).

One of the most magnificent testimonies to human weakness was found in the denial of Peter. His weakness, however, became his strength. I am sure Peter never forgot that he was the Apostle who had openly denied the Lord. But Peter also knew that because he was so weak, because he lived with the limitation of being an impetuous man, the Lord loved him dearly. The Lord loved him in his weakness and not in his strength. The proud Peter, the one who claimed that he would be with the Lord to the bitter end, crumbled. The Rock became like the rest of men, a broken vessel of clay. After the Resurrection and in the event of Pentecost, Christ filled this vessel with the priceless treasure of the Holy Spirit. In his woundedness, Peter finally became genuinely open to Christ, and I have the impression that, if Peter were alive today, he would be a gentle priest to whom many could easily talk.

---

34. Refer to *Personal Care and Pastoral Presence,* pp. 297-303, in which I discuss Piet Schoonenberg's theological teaching on the mystery of man as sinner.

How gentle am I with my people? Christ said: "Come to me, all you who labor and are overburdened, and I will give you rest. Shoulder my yoke and learn from me, for I am gentle and humble in heart, and you will find rest for your souls. Yes my yoke is easy and my burden light." (Matt. 11:28-30). How different this value system is when compared with the competitive value system that is so often prevalent in our society today. No one of us is an island all to himself. Life is not the survival of the fittest; it is a situatedness in woundedness. Henri Nouwen writes beautifully and clearly on this wounded kind of gentle presence in the life of the pastoral minister.[35] As a parish priest, I am able to be a caring and healing presence to people only when I am there with them in a common woundedness, a shared vulnerability. As a priest I do not save anyone. I am called to be with people, to let my life enter into theirs and let their life enter into mine. Life becomes a common search, and true parish community creates a unity based on the confession of our basic brokenness and a shared hope. The Christian parish is a healing community not because wounds are cured and all pains are alleviated, but because wounds and pains become openings or occasions for a new vision. Our common hope leads us far beyond the boundaries of human togetherness to a Christ who calls his people away from the land of slavery into a land of genuine paschal liberation, from the immanent toward the transcendent.

When I visit sick persons in the hospital, I cannot take away their cancer. I cannot make them safe and secure. I cannot take away the grief of loved ones when a beloved member of their family dies. I cannot rescue the countless lonely people who live in the parish nursing homes or who live alone in many of our parish homes. I cannot remove suffering, for suffering in many

---

35. Henri J. M. Nouwen, *Creative Ministry* (Garden City, NY: Doubleday & Co., 1971); *The Wounded Healer* (Garden City, NY: Doubleday & Co., 1972); *Reaching Out* (Garden City, NY; Doubleday & Co., 1975).

various ways is interwoven into the tapestry of everyday life. Suffering is a limit situation that always points beyond itself.[36] Jesus understood this fact when he made his own broken body the way to health, to liberation, and to new life. He did not take suffering away but shared completely in the poverty of man's brokenness. His death pointed to resurrection and new life. His suffering and death were not the total horizon of Christ. As a parish priest, I am called to share this reality of Christ's life as a present condition of my own life. My woundedness is not something I can hide. It points beyond itself. It is not an experience I can refuse to accept as present in my life. I too can be lonely. I too can lose a loved one in death. I too can be sick and ill, weak, confused, and upset. I do not thus become a spiritual exhibitionist and walk around with open wounds that merely "stink" and do not heal. Making my own wounds a source of healing does not call for a sharing of superficial pain but a constant willingness to see our common pain and suffering as rising from the depths of the broken human condition that all men share.

A MAN CALLED TO LEAD

Andrew Greeley makes the distinction between an "instrumental" leader and an "expressive" leader.[37] The instrumental leader is one whose primary concern is getting things done: the fulfillment of tasks, organization, administration, and implementation. He is a doer, a planner, a decision maker. The expressive leader, on the other hand, is more concerned with the overall picture and with the people he leads. He makes sure that the visions of the community are clear and that the morale of its members is high. He soothes over hurt feelings, reassures the

36. Refer to *Personal Care and Pastoral Presence,* pp. 120-21, in which I discuss Bernard J. Boelen's understanding of limit situations which point beyond the immediate experience to a transcendent mystery.
37. Andrew Greeley, *New Horizons for the Priesthood* (New York, NY: Sheed and Ward, Inc., 1970), pp. 48-60.

troubled, encourages the weary, makes peace between the angry, and inspires the discouraged. Pope John XXIII was a living example of an expressive leader.

A parish pastor has very often been measured by what he does. He has been an "administrator" or an instrumental leader who lives functionally and efficiently by "doing." The expressive leader is, however, a man who "is." In suggesting that parishes need more expressive leaders as pastors, I am not saying that all administrative functions can be most effectively delegated or practically placed under the supervision of committees, the parish council, or diocesan pastoral councils. A pastor will often need to be a wise and balanced harmony of both leadership models. He cannot inspire and reassure, he cannot love and care for people, he cannot move the minds and hearts of men merely by efficient administration or committee delegation. The genuine pastor leads by balancing the immanent dynamic of instrumental leadership with the transcendent quality of expressive vision.

The wonderful thing about a parish is that the priests are not the only ones to whom the Holy Spirit gives certain gifts. Multiple spiritual gifts are given to the whole community. Various people in the parish bring different gifts to the whole parish family, and all members work together for the good of the entire body. This cooperation is the theological reality of parish life. What is necessary, then, is that the priest become a director of ministries, a true spiritual leader of active Christians rather than the only person in the parish or the given apostolate expected to manifest spiritual initiative. The living Christ is working in the midst of his parish people. The people are indeed the Christ who serves the priest in a way that complements the priest's ministry of Christ to them. Therefore, I must learn to stand in the midst of my people, gratefully receiving and humbly coordinating the action of the Spirit to bring to perfect maturity this small cell of the Body of Christ. I immediately think of the leader of an

orchestra. He does not compose the symphony but leads by calling forth the various instruments to play in an integrated and
graceful harmony. In a similar sense, the parish priest directs the
various gifts of the Divine Composer found in different individ-
uals and in the common movements of daily life.

I am thus advocating a whole new reversal for many of us as
priests. The new style of expressive leadership is to be "with"
my people rather than always "out in front" of them. Granted,
this call to break out of the old style of parish priesthood where
everyone listened to Father is transcendent and disturbing.
Father must now more and more listen to his people. He meets
Christ and receives the care of Christ in his people. The
priesthood of the faithful, which is fundamentally present
through baptism, anoints Father with the presence of Christ.
The parish family is a priestly people who share priesthood with
one another. As a result, trusting openness becomes the fundamental meaning of a parish priest's celibacy. I am suggesting
here that the gift of celibacy is not given to me for myself but for
the sake of the development of the parish community that is entrusted to me. It is not given to me so that I may dominate
others. Celibate ministry is a serving gift that calls forth the
various gifts of the parish family. Thus parish councils, team
ministries, staff meetings of all those responsibly involved in
parish life, and, in fact, any interpersonal relationships I may
have in my parish experience are all opportunities to watch over
and shepherd the meaning that God has placed before me and
not the meaning I project as "the way."

LIVING THE SPIRIT OF THE
EVANGELICAL COUNSELS

Pope John XXIII in his encyclical letter, *Sacerdotii Nostri
Primordia,* offers Saint John Vianney, the Cure of Ars, as an example for all priests, particularly in his practice of the
evangelical counsels, his prayer life, and his pastoral ministry.

Pope John indicates that the diocesan parish priest is not called to live the evangelical counsels by canonical vows. However, he does encourage all parish priests to live the spirit of the counsels:

> Our predecessor of happy memory, Pius XII, in order to give a clear picture of his doctrine and to clear up doubts and errors that bothered some people, denied that "the clerical state—as such, and on the basis of divine law—requires, of its very nature or at least as a result of some demand arising from its nature that those enrolled in it observe the evangelical counsels" and concluded with these words: "Hence a cleric is not bound by virtue of divine law to the evangelical counsels of poverty, chastity, obedience."
>
> And yet it would undoubtedly be both a distortion of the real mind of this same Supreme Pontiff (who was so interested in the sanctity of the clergy) and a contradiction of the perpetual teaching of the Church in this matter, if anyone should dare to infer from this that clerics were any less bound by their office than religious to strive for evangelical perfection of life. The truth is just the opposite; for the proper exercise of the priestly functions "requires a greater interior holiness than is demanded by the religious state" (cf. Pius XII, Allocution, April 16, 1953: A A S 45 [1953] 288). And even if churchmen are not commanded to embrace these evangelical counsels by virtue of their clerical state, it still remains true that in their efforts to achieve holiness, these counsels offer them and all of the faithful the surest road to the desired goal of perfection.[38]

Adrian van Kaam traces this threefold path back to the animal kingdom.[39] The survival of every animal was dependent on the adaptive process. In order to survive, animals were, and still are, instinctively obedient to the conditions of their natural environment. Van Kaam uses the term obedience in its original Latin sense, which is *ob-audire,* meaning "to listen to." Through "listening," animals learn to adapt, survive, and evolve. For example, dark-skinned bears turned white with the coming of the ice age. Secondly, an animal can survive only if he

---

38. Pope John XXIII, The Encyclical Letter, *Sacerdotii Nostri Primordia, The Pope Speaks* (Washington, D.C., 1959), p. 11.
39. Adrian van Kaam, *Personality Fulfillment in the Spiritual Life* (Wilkes-Barre, PA: Dimension Books, 1966), pp. 154-84.

lives with others like himself and can come together in herds or groups. A lonely animal is doomed. He needs the group. His survival depends on affective togetherness. There is thus an instinctive togetherness or gregariousness found in the animal kingdom. There is also a built-in instinct of moderation that enables animals not to impose unduly upon others. This instinctive "respect" is observed in the fact that animals of the same species will care for one another and seldom destroy one another if the proper "survival space" is preserved and protected. Of course, if this spatial or "territorial imperative" is trespassed, then aggression may occur. Thirdly, an animal must use his environment correctly and in moderation. The squirrel hoards nuts in order to survive the winter. Yet his built-in instinct tells him when to stop, when to moderate his need. He does not gather nuts continually. He has an instinctively controlled sense of "poverty." At the human level, these instinctive conditions for evolution in the animal kingdom are not destroyed. In man, the threefold path becomes a spirited and free obedience, respectful chastity, and poverty.

As a parish priest, I am called to live the spirit of these three counsels. Large groups, as van Kaam points out, do not take significant steps forward in the evolution of mankind. Rather, small groups living in special conditions lead the way. These small groups are witnesses to the rest of the population. They inspire others to go forward. In all histories we find small special groups in the intellectual realm, in the art world, in the freedom movement, in the religious milieu, who show the way. Religious communities witness religious value to the wider world by the canonical vows of obedience, chastity, and poverty. They radiate religious value by their living witness. The parish priest is called to live this threefold way without taking canonical vows. Obedience becomes the virtue of being able to listen and hear what is going on in my life. I listen to the original rhythms of my own vital, personal, and spiritual levels. By listening to who I am and who I am called to become in God's providence, I become my real self and not merely a person living a role. I learn to listen to the original and gifted presence of the others who are entrusted to me. I listen to the bishop in whose diocese I serve. I listen in prayer to the whispered intimations of God himself. As a chaste man, I am able to offer my celibacy as a trusting openness to the service of the parish community. I do not build exclusive relationships with a few people or with a single one, as is the case in marriage. Rather, my personal relationships with others are nonexclusive and respectful. My celibacy leaves me open to all people living in the parish community. I am able to let the other be uniquely and originally other than I. I do not have to use, manipulate, or control the people of my parish. I have a vision that "sees again" into the deep mystery of reality. The word respect comes from the Latin word *re-spicere,* meaning "to look or see again." Finally, in my relationship to the things of my world, I live with a spirit of poverty when I respectfully see and use all things in moderation.

If I live the genuine spirit of the threefold way, I become a witness to the people of my parish. I witness to the transcendent. I am able to listen to events, respectfully relate to people, and moderately use things against and pointing to the deeper horizon of God's presence. In other words, my presence to the events of history, people, and things is not only a free presence to their immediate appearances but also a presence to their transcendent value. I become the man who no longer loses himself in merely the immanent surface meaning of life. I become the transcendent disturber, the one who, in the image of the Almighty Father, calls people forth to new life in Jesus Christ.

Is it not interesting that Jesus remarks to Martha that there is new life for the man who believes in Him, even if he dies? But Jesus goes even further. He says, "Whoever lives and believes in me will never die" (John 11:26). To live in obedience, chastity, and poverty, and to believe that these three great counsels are rooted in Jesus Christ, is to live a life that never dies. Such a priest, such a person, can never merely be the safe one, the immanently closed one. For this man, life is a journey into future possibilities. The transcendent man is the pilgrim as well as the good shepherd who watches over his parish and cares for a pilgrim people; he does so knowing that ultimately:

> The Lord is my shepherd;
>   I shall not want.
> In verdant pastures he gives me repose;
>   beside restful waters he leads me;
>   he refreshes my soul.
> He guides me in right paths for his name's sake.
> Even though I walk in the dark valley I fear no evil;
>   for you are at my side with your rod and your
>   staff that give me courage.
>
> You spread the table before me in the sight of my foes;
>   you anoint my head with oil;
>   my cup overflows.
> Only goodness and kindness follow me all the days
>   of my life;
>   and I shall dwell in the house of the Lord for
>   years to come.[40]

SUMMARY

In this chapter, I have looked at the immanent and transcendent dynamics of a parish priest's life. I have tried to explore facilitating conditions that could enable a priest to move from immanence to transcendence. I have considered caring time for personal friendship with priest associates; caring time to be prayerfully present to God; caring time to be personally present with others in my parish; rectory living in a genuine caring space; the attitudes of leisure, playfulness, wonder, and gentleness; instrumental and expressive leadership; and caring to live the spirit of the evangelical counsels of obedience, chastity, and poverty.

---

40. *New American Catholic Edition of The Holy Bible,* Confraternity Edition (New York, NY: Benzinger Brothers, Inc., 1950), pp. 541-42, Psalm 22.

APPENDIX

A SPIRITUAL MEDITATION
ON JOHN THE BAPTIST[1]

In the beginning was the Word. . . .
He was with God in the beginning.
Through him all things came to be,
not one thing had its being but through him.
All that came to be had life in him
and that life was the light of men,
a light that shines in the dark,
a light that darkness could not overpower.

(John 1:1-5)[2]

Seminary life and spiritual formation are truly a new beginning, not only for the seminarian, but also for the spiritual director. In Saint John's prologue I learn that in the very beginning was the Word and that through the Word all things came to be. My very being, my whole life rests, ultimately, in the Word. When I come to the seminary as a spiritual director or as a seminarian, I must realize that such a new beginning lives always in the beginning of the Word. Christ himself is always there with me in every moment of my life. I am never alone or isolated, for life is a series of new beginnings that, ultimately, rests in the beginning mystery of the Lord.

---

1. For the ideas expressed in this spiritual reflection I am indebted to Adrian van Kaam's meditative reflections on the Gospel of Saint John. These reflections were given in van Kaam's unpublished class notes, Fall Semester, 1974, Lectures I, III, IV, V, VI, VII, VIII, XIV. These lectures were given at the Center for the Study of Spirituality of the Institute of Man at Duquesne University, Pittsburgh, PA.
2. All scriptural references in this appendix are taken from *The Jerusalem Bible* (Garden City, NY: Doubleday and Co., 1971).

A WITNESS TO SPEAK FOR THE LIGHT OF CHRIST

A man came sent by God.
His name was John.
He came as a witness,
as a witness to speak for the light,
so that everyone might believe through him.
He was not the light,
only a witness to speak for the light.

(John 1:6-8)

In the prologue, John points out that John the Baptist was sent by God as a witness to speak for the light. He was not the light but only a witness to speak for the light. Only the Word was the true light. The place of the spiritual director in the seminary is the call to become another John the Baptist. God places him as an important person in the spiritual formation of young seminarians. Therefore, I am called also to be a witness to the light of Christ. I am not the light but I am called to lead people to the true light. This consideration is important because we all live in a world of spiritual darkness. We are so often fallen away from our true originality. We can be so easily lost in the superficial "little words" or superficial meanings of our day-to-day world. My vital and personal levels many times take over in my life, and I become lost in a world that totalizes partial or "little beyonds" into the "Big Beyond."[3] I become blind to my deeper spiritual self as the meeting place for the divine light. I do not hear the divine call to become who I am uniquely and originally called to be by the Original Source of all life.[4]

As a witness to the light of Christ and not to my own little lights, which often become favorite little ideologies, I point

---

3. Refer to *Personal Care and Pastoral Presence,* pp. 14-15. Here I discuss van Kaam's consideration of man's tendency to totalize partial wholes.

4. Refer to *Personal Care and Pastoral Presence,* pp. 12-16, in which I discuss van Kaam's concept of spiritual personality and man's tendency to totalize partial wholes. Refer also to pp. 106-109, in which I discuss van Kaam's understanding of personal originality.

always to Christ. This realization is liberating, for I no longer have to pretend to know everything. I can let the light of Christ be ultimately responsible for the spiritual direction of my own life as well as the lives of the seminarians. I am merely a humble instrument of the Lord, not the Lord himself. I can begin to admit my own insignificance and not unnecessarily worry about people discovering it.

When Christ entered the history of the world, the world was filled with darkness and did not know the Word. The world still does not know the Word. However, the Word is in everything and has ownership over every creature. Every person, event, or thing I touch, see, hear, or meet in my day-to-day world is already touched, seen, heard, and met by the Word. In becoming flesh, Christ literally came into his own, a world owned by the Eternal Word from the very beginning. If I can say yes to his ownership and not to my own, then the meeting place of spiritual director and seminarian becomes the tenting place of the Lord, the shekinah of God's presence with his people. Such can happen only when I entrust my own will to God's will, when I live in a day-to-day world that is always and providentially his world and not my own. As a spiritual director, I am no longer master but servant and steward over the precious gift of life that God has entrusted to me and the gift of unique and original life he has entrusted to young seminarians.

THE SEMINARIAN IS A UNIQUE AND ORIGINAL PERSON IN CHRIST; HE RANKS BEFORE ME

When John appeared as witness he proclaimed: "This is the one of whom I said, 'He who comes after me ranks before me because he existed before me'" (John 1:15). This consideration is important for a spiritual director. Each seminarian who comes into my life is originally called by God to be his unique self. Spiritual direction is not a mechanical system of formation that stamps out carbon copy candidates. The word formation suggests more than an exterior shaping. The very root of the word is found in the Latin word *forma,* which means "the essential quality or nature of a thing as distinguished from the matter in which it is embodied."[5] True spiritual formation should be interested in cultivating and fostering conditions that enable the seminarian to unfold as a unique and original person in Christ. Each seminarian is truly one who comes after me but ranks before me because he is in truth an emerging Christ. Essentially, the seminarian is a unique and original unfolding of the mystery of Christ before me.

When I am tempted to think that the seminarian is so young, so inexperienced, so foolish at times, so different from me or my contemporaries who have more experience in the priesthood, it is good to refresh my memory with these words of John the Baptist. I can humbly listen and see a magnificent mystery emerging in a seminarian. In him Christ is present before me in a unique and original way. If I can have confidence in Christ, then I can have confidence and faith in the many who are coming after me in the priesthood. The future will hold in store many new experiences and ways that have not been my ways. The beauty of Christ is his emergence in universality and not uniformity. The future seminarians are called to be universal ministers of the Lord's presence. They will touch, see, hear, and meet experiences in this world that I know nothing of. They will relate to and assist people whom I could never touch or understand. Yet, as John the Baptist understood so well, this stepping aside to let the Lord emerge in new ways is an important condition of spiritual poverty befitting the witness who points to the Lord and not to himself.

MAKE A STRAIGHT WAY FOR THE LORD

When people asked John the Baptist who he was, he did not pretend to be other than he was. He declared openly that he was

---

5. *Webster's New International Dictionary* (Springfield, MA: G. & C. Merriam Co., 1955), p. 991.

not the Christ, or Elijah, or one of the prophets. He merely quoted and lived the prophecy of Isaiah: "I am a voice that cries in the wilderness: Make a straight way for the Lord" (John 1:23). John could say this about himself because he knew that all people already have in themselves a voice that cries in the wilderness for the Lord. He realized that man is a spirit person. But man is a spirit in a fallen flesh, in a fallen body. John's spirit, my own spirit, and the spirit of a seminarian are voices that have to cry out because they are not heard. They are not heard because man's fallen being is like a wilderness or a desert.

I am often afraid of the spirit because it takes me out of my complacent consistency in a taken-for-granted world I think I can control. I am usually more comfortable living in the daily desert of my worldly existence. I am often completely enmeshed there. I lose the beautiful horizon of the Holy in my life, for it is too risky to give up my self-centered existence.

From time to time, however, I may experience that my life is a wilderness. I can become aware of living in the quiet desperation of a dispirited life. My difficulty is that I hesitate to listen and look deeply at my despair. I try to tell myself that the desert is not really a desert but an oasis full of life. Such a repression of spirit leads to a life of illusion. But the voice of my spirit keeps crying out, "Make a straight way for the Lord." It calls me to clear out the false idols of my life, such idols as being a social success, being accepted, getting ahead, and so on. The voice of spirit urges me to make the way straight for the Lord so that the Lord, who speaks in and through the spirit, can come to live more deeply in my total life experience. It encourages me to let the Lord emerge in my life in the unique and original way his Father has called me to become and not in the way the world calls me to be.

The natural spirit of a man is a magnificent mystery. It is only that voice crying in the day-to-day wilderness of life that enables the apostolate, ministry, and preaching to be effective. No apostolate, no preaching, no ministry, no person could ever be effective if there were not already, in those addressed by the witness, a similar voice crying, a repressed awareness that life is a desert, that life can be desperate. As a witness to the Lord, I am magnifying the inner voice of the spirit that speaks in all people who live around me. As a witness, I may have a double reception. Some people will welcome me; others will be anxious and even avoid me. This double reception can exist in the same person and often will contextualize many of the relationships a spiritual director may have with seminarians. When others openly recognize the voice of the spirit, they will welcome it. When they repress the voice of the spirit, they will experience anxiety. I need not become upset with the anxiety of those who feel uncomfortable in my presence, for I am only a witness of a pre-existent inner Christ who is slowly working in the other's natural spirit according to his hour and not my hour.

WAITING ON THE PRESENCE OF THE LORD

The beauty of John the Baptist was that he waited on the presence and hour of the Lord. In him is symbolized the faithful waiting of the Jewish people, the Levites, a symbol of all of mankind waiting for the Christ to emerge. They did not know what the Christ really was or what he would be like. They only knew from the prophets that there would be an advent of the Messiah. In the chosen people, the natural spirit of man was opened up indirectly in reaching for Christ. However, at times in salvation history, man has tended to deflate his spiritual striving to something that is less than Christ. People have tended to deify a model person to take the place of Christ.

THE DANGER OF TRANSFERENCE

Transference was a great danger for John the Baptist. He was a powerful and striking witness. He had lived in the desert. He was a great preacher, and many were impressed by him. The dynamic of human transference quite naturally occurred. John initially became the ideal. John must be the Christ. In such a milieu, John humbly declared "quite openly," "I am not the Christ" (John 1:20). Transference also can become a difficult dynamic in seminary formation. The spiritual director is the witness who should be ready to make the way straight for the Lord in the lives of seminarians. However, if the director does not make it very clear that he is only a witness for Christ, then he can become enmeshed in a situation in which seminarians transfer their attention and love for Christ to the director. The director can allow his ways to become their ways, his knowledge their knowledge, his personal or special devotions their personal or special devotions.[6]

THE WAY OF PREPARATION

Therefore, the mature spiritual director must always keep the model of John the Baptist before him. I am not the one. I am merely a voice that magnifies the inner voice of natural spirit that is already present in the candidate. I call that inner voice of the seminarian to make a straight way in his own wilderness and dryness. I appeal to the deeper voice of the Lord's presence given to him in his baptism, the life of grace. John goes on to tell the people: "I baptize with water; but there stands among you—unknown to you—the one who is coming after me; and I am not fit to undo his sandal strap. . . ." (John 1:26-28). John is saying that his witness is a kind of external, symbolic washing. It cannot be compared with what would happen if people would truly open up to Christ and the baptism of the Holy Spirit. John's baptism, like the relationship of a spiritual director and a seminarian, is a preparing of the way for the Unknown One who always stands in our midst. Spiritual director and directee can

6. Adrian van Kaam, *In Search of Spiritual Identity* (Denville, NJ: Dimension Books, 1975), pp. 7-30. In this extremely important book, van Kaam makes the distinction between fundamental, special, and personal Catholic spirituality. Refer also to *Personal Care and Pastoral Presence,* pp. 530-36, in which I elaborate on this distinction.

thus be seen as advent persons who wait together in the presence of the Lord.

THE WAY OF HUMBLE PRESENCE:
TO NOT CARE IN ORDER TO CARE

As spiritual director, I am not even fit to undo his sandal strap. John lived totally for Christ and not for himself. Such faith is the kind both director and seminarian need in their encounter with one another. We can do absolutely nothing for ourselves. As director, I can baptize with the water of preparation. I can suggest conditions that foster a deeper openness to the coming of the Holy Spirit. Only the Holy Spirit, however, can deepen the baptism of preparing for new life in the Spirit. No matter how much I have learned, studied, and experienced in life, I am still not fit to undo his sandal strap. There is a great deal to meditate on here, for undoing a sandal strap is a simple and humble thing. I have to bend before someone else. And yet John the Baptist says that he is not even fit to do such a simple thing. He reminds me of how unworthy I am and how important Christ really is in spiritual growth and formation.

The totality of John's witness always rested against the background or horizon of the Eternal Word. John was a man filled with awe, a man who realized that he was nothing and that Christ was everything. John is not an easy model to imitate, for most men do not want to be nothing. My pride system is always getting in the way. I like to think that I am very important. I can often think that I know the best way for a seminarian to follow. Only a constant and disciplined desert preparation in my own life will enable me to point to the Lord and not to myself. This preparation includes a faithful practice of daily meditation, prayer, and spiritual reading. It means looking and listening to the wilderness of my life, recognizing how fallen I can be in tendencies to live in the illusory oases of my own vital and personal levels. The more I begin to have the faith and awe of John the Baptist, the more I will be able to be a simple witness to Christ. The more I am in the way, the more important I feel, the less chance there is for grace to flow into seminarians. Not being worthy to undo even His sandal strap is to learn to not care in order to care, to become the humble opening through which Christ meets his chosen ones.

THE WAY OF THE LAMB

The fundamental question concerns itself with who the Christ is. The evangelist John continues his Gospel by saying: "The next day, seeing Jesus coming toward him, John said, 'Look, there is the lamb of God that takes away the sin of this world. . . .'" (John 1:29). John sees Jesus coming toward him. This coming had to be the high point of his life. He certainly did not have the same insight we now have through Revelation. However, he knew intuitively that the lamb of God was the greatest event that ever happened to the world. John's whole life had been a preparation for this moment, and his witness was a proclamation of preparation to the hearts and souls of the people. The lamb of God image means that the Lord does not come as a great scholar, as a victorious person, or as a great leader. John is proclaiming the poverty of the Lord. God is really poor and helpless in my world. He is so infinitely considerate of my freedom that in no way does he impose himself on me. He does not force or control me through power. In every way he leaves me free. He comes as the defenseless and helpless one.

The image of the lamb speaks to my own helplessness and utter vulnerability when I have the tendency to hide in a defensive and aggressive attitude. Because I am human, I too like to overcome my fear of impotence and powerlessness by showing others and myself that I am in complete control. This behavior occurs in me as a spiritual director when I forget that I am not the Lord but merely the witness to the Lord. I may isolate myself from his ways and substitute my own. I can become tense and worried.

Many times I can find it humanly difficult to be like a lamb. Yet the Lord is called the lamb. In every Eucharist that I celebrate, I proclaim, as John the Baptist did, "See the lamb who takes away the sins of the world."

This raises the question of what really is the sin of the world. Man is constantly shadowed by an original terror.[7] Because I am spirit, I am terrified of opening up to the transcendent. By seeing myself in the light of all that is, I begin to see my smallness, my helplessness, my vulnerability. In order to overcome this feeling of original terror, I will tend to close myself off from the spiritually transcendent perspective. I may try to become relevant and important in all kinds of little ways. Of course, the world I live in will be more than glad to help me by inventing all kinds of social games in which I can gain status and recognition. Such is the sin of the world. I tend to close myself off from a transcendentally unique and original relevancy with God and substitute for it a closed and safe way of being relevant in the world by looking good on its terms. I substitute the immanent dimension for the transcendent and make some "little beyond" the "Big Beyond" of my life.

Now it is difficult to overcome this sin of the world; in fact, it is impossible on my own power. I need grace.[8] Grace comes to me through Jesus Christ who comes as the lamb of God who takes away the sin of the world. The lamb takes away the sin of the world not only through His suffering and death but by being the concrete model who exemplifies how we must not be aggressive and defensive. We must, instead, be open in the relaxed surrender of a lamb. Only when I am like a lamb and not like a lion does the Divine love me and lift me up in grace. As a lamb, I can begin to become relaxed, gentle, quiet, patient, attentive, and watchful for His presence in my life.

---

7. Refer to *Personal Care and Pastoral Presence,* pp. 96-100, in which I discuss van Kaam's understanding of original terror.

8. Refer to *Personal Care and Pastoral Presence,* pp. 315-25, wherein I discuss Peter Fransen's understanding of the mystery of grace.

This is why John could continue to say: "This is the one I spoke of when I said: A man is coming after me who ranks before me because he existed before me" (John 1:30). John saw the lamb against the background of the Eternal Divine pre-existence as the Eternal Word. The meek and surrendering lamb ranks before all of us because He existed before us. This simple man walking toward John was pre-existent from all eternity. He was and is God.

THE WAY OF NOT KNOWING

John says: "I did not know him myself, and yet it was to reveal him to Israel that I came baptizing with water" (John 1:31). How true this statement is for anyone in spiritual direction. As a spiritual director, I am coming to witness for Christ. Yet, I must say I do not completely know him myself. I can know "of" him and "about" him but I cannot ever know him fully. I can know some of him. Sometimes he will reveal himself to my heart. But I can never say that I know him fully. I must always be humble and trustingly open enough to admit this truth. Not fully knowing is important for me to consider because, in my association with seminarians, I will find wonderful new manifestations of Jesus' presence. I can be struck by such a new presence and realize that I did not know that Christ could or would work this way. I must learn to live in a humility of knowing and not knowing. The moment I lose this humility and say that I know him, I can no longer discover him anew in all the events and people of my life.

Seminarians and some directors can adopt a theological perspective that attempts to "figure out" the Lord and say that it knows him. Of course, we can know about God intellectually, and this knowing is good and important. What is dangerous is the attitude that believes such knowledge is all there is to knowing the Lord. Experientially, I never stop in life. Life is not static but dynamic. Life flows or unfolds out of the past into the present and on into the future. The longer I live, the more I realize how very little I know. This healthy attitude will emerge in my life if I remain humbly open to the mystery of life. The more I can live this awareness of not knowing, the more I can be like a child who eagerly waits and hungers to know more of life's mystery. This deep desire for the Lord can come only when I realize that I do not know. When I feel that I know something, I really have no burning desire to attain it. I take it for granted, and it becomes part of my complacent "asleepness" in the world. John the Baptist was certainly not "asleep" in knowing but "wide awake" in his not knowing, and the latter made all the difference in his life. So it must be in the life of any spiritual director or seminarian.

THE PRIDE OF KNOWING

One of the real dangers in spiritual direction is that after one has done it for quite awhile, one can become quite good. One can begin to live with the creeping pride of knowing the Lord. The more this attitude pervades one's life, the less effective one will be as a channel of the Lord's presence. This attitude of knowing vs. not knowing may often be present in the minds of those who choose spiritual directors for seminaries. Usually a priest who has been successfully situated in a parish setting will be chosen. We think this particular priest knows because he was trained in a seminary and has had good experience in parish life. Because we foolishly trust that this priest knows, we feel no need to train him in not knowing. A seminary may expend all kinds of money and energy sending future faculty members off for study in many different disciplines. But this same seminary assumes that the spiritual director's position can be filled immediately by transferring a priest from parish life into full-time spiritual direction. We say that spiritual direction is important and that spiritual life is the most fundamental part of a priest's life; yet we do scarcely anything to uncover and train sensitive people for this job.

As typically Western men, we may pride ourselves on knowing what the priesthood and spiritual life are all about. In recent times, consequently, we may have reaped the harvest of many ordained priests' leaving the priesthood basically because they had no strong experiential foundation in the spiritual life. They were trained in seminaries where spiritual formation was a "knowing about" spiritual life. Too often they were not exposed to the actual lived experience of a spiritual life that was fundamentally in tune with their original and unique selves as well as with the fundamental Catholic doctrine of the Church.

When the Church and those who make responsible decisions about the future of the Church come to meditate on and begin to live seriously this "not knowing" attitude of John the Baptist, we can achieve a new beginning in Christ's presence, and we need not remain embedded in our own ego-oriented ways. The Eastern spiritual master, who sometimes smiles at us in the West and gently reminds us that "not knowing" is the beginning of true knowing, echoes the model of John the Baptist's presence. With deeper reflection, we might begin to realize that there is no such phenomenon as an "instant" spiritual director. Such "practical" solutions bespeak a lack of critical reflection about the mystery of life. Life growth is a process that takes considerable time and experience to unfold. It cannot be merely another problem that we attack and answer with the controling "handles" of an ego orientation.

OPENNESS TO THE HOLY SPIRIT

John also declares: "I saw the Spirit coming down on him from heaven like a dove and resting on him. I did not know him myself, but he who sent me to baptize with water had said to me, 'The man on whom you see the Spirit come down and rest is the one who is going to baptize with the Holy Spirit.' Yes, I have seen, and I am the witness that he is the Chosen One of God" (John 1:32-34). In this statement we find the beautiful role of the Holy Spirit. My human spirit is that core center of my being in which I am already naturally in tune with the wider pattern of the universe. John is proclaiming that the natural spirit, the universe, the pattern of the universe is permeated with the Holy Spirit who is truly God. My natural spiritual unfolding is rooted in the openness of my spirit to the Holy Spirit. In Jesus is manifested the Spirit that comes down and rests. Jesus is the one who baptizes in the Spirit. The great sign for John was that the Holy Spirit did come down and rest on the Lord. This is a sign for all of us in spiritual direction. We must allow the Holy Spirit to rest in our lives, in our spirits. To the degree that we are open to the Holy Spirit, we are truly inspired or in-spirited. Baptism is not merely baptism with water but a baptism with the Holy Spirit. The Holy Spirit is always ready to come, if only we allow him into our lives.

In baptism, I have also become a Chosen One of God. The spiritual director's call is a further elaboration or specification of God's original call in baptism. He is chosen to be in formation so that, like John the Baptist, he can witness to the life of the Holy Spirit coming down and resting not only in his own life but in the lives of seminarians who are especially chosen by God. John recognized the Spirit because he was a man who prepared himself for this moment by a disciplined life of prayer, meditation, and penance. And so must a spiritual director prepare. A great deal of time and space must be given over to preparing for the coming of the Holy Spirit. Prayer, reflection, study, spiritual reading, and meditation must become important ways of "going into the desert" so that the Jordan experience may again happen gracefully in a director's homilies, conferences, counseling, and direction.

POINTING TO THE LAMB

The story of John's witness continues:

On the following day as John stood there again with two of his disciples, Jesus passed, and John stared at him hard and said,

> "Look, there is the lamb of God." Hearing this, the two
> disciples followed Jesus. Jesus turned around, saw them
> following, and said, "What do you want?" They answered,
> "Rabbi,"—which means Teacher—"where do you live?"
> "Come and see," he replied; so they went and saw where he
> lived, and stayed with him the rest of the day. . . .
>   (John 1:35-39)

Again, we have the strong personality of John saying the same thing about the Lord, "Look, there is the lamb of God." Christ came into our world as the powerless one. The question is why. The answer lies in my constant refusal to admit my own utter vulnerability, my total helplessness, my total powerlessness. I do not usually aspire to be a lamb, and the same can be said for most seminarians. Being a lamb is not too exciting or spectacular. Lambs do not usually change the course of history. In fact, lambs are truly powerless, tiny, and always running back to their mothers when we observe them in a pasture. John the Baptist knew about lambs, and yet he called Christ the lamb of God. If John were to have been more like a "relevant" twentieth century man, he would have introduced his disciples to a strong Christ. Such an introduction is the accepted way of our world. If I introduce people to someone I want them to follow, I tell them how strong, heroic, clever, or relevant such a person is. John the Baptist does exactly the opposite. Christ is worthwhile because he is God, but, from the human viewpoint, John is saying He is like a lamb, powerless, meek, not impressive at all.

How difficult it must have been for the disciples of John to understand this introduction. John himself was a powerful man. He was scarcely thought of as being meek and helpless. And yet this strong man pointed out that the true way is the way of the new man, the way of the lamb. John was strong enough to be weak and gentle.

WHERE DO YOU LIVE?

The disciples began to follow Jesus, and he asked them what they wanted. This question is quite symbolic of a young man who is beginning to search seriously into his vocation. The disciples, like seminarians, ask Him, "Where do you live?" This question is profound; it has deep spiritual meaning. The disciples are not merely asking about the physical place that Jesus called home; they are asking Jesus about the center of his life. In modern language we might say, "Jesus, what makes you tick? Who are you? We are curious about a man who comes as a lamb. You are a 'Rabbi'; so teach us your way."

Where a person lives is an interesting sign. It tells me something about who the person is. Where and how I live signifies or shows something of who I am. It exteriorizes that which lives in me as my fundamental care or concern. As a spiritual director or as a seminarian, I may "sacramentalize" my inner world by the way I appoint and arrange my room, the books I choose to read, the music I care to listen to, the way I study and organize my life, the presence I am in prayer and liturgical celebration, and so on. Where and how I live often may tell me what is important for me. The concrete "where" and "how" of my life could imply the deeper "where" and "what" of the kind of world of care, love, and ideals I am living. If, for example, my room is filled to overflowing with congestion and disarray, I might ponder whether this "outer" world indicates something significant concerning my "inner" world. If I am seeking a simple life of prayerful peace, my outer world should begin to reflect the harmony of my inner search. Such can be said for both director and seminarian.

THE SEMINARY IS A PLACE APART
FROM AND OPEN TO THE WORLD

Jesus replied: "Come and see!" The disciples went and saw where he lived and stayed with him the rest of the day. Like the first disciples, we are all called to come and see where he lives. This calling is the whole meaning of seminary life. The seminary is a place where we are invited by the Lord to come and see where he lives in a deeply caring way. We should understand the seminary as an originating experience, a place where study, reflection, prayerful meditation, and reflective spiritual reading cultivates the unique seed of being called to the priesthood of Christ.

In the seminary, the spiritual director is always encouraging the candidates to look at and see the lamb of God. The seminary is not supposed to become the most exciting place in the world. No one is going to find himself front page news when he is living in the seminary. It should be a place apart from the world in which a young man can truly meet the lamb. I do not suggest that we go back to the old seminary tradition in which candidates for a future ministry in the world were completely held apart from any meaningful engagement and learning experiences in the world. The problem today is exactly the opposite. It might be suggested that the seminarian is too much involved with the social apostolate in the world. What is necessary in diocesan seminary life is the challenge to find a happy balance between being involved and being detached.[9]

The Church of the future does not have to worry about whether it will find its future priests open to social action and theological maturity. Their training in these areas is excellent. It can be anxious, however, about whether its future priests are deeply spiritual men. The average parishioner in today's world is hungering for more than a priest who is a disguised social worker, proclaiming the human development of man. The priest should be naturally concerned for human development, but the pivotal reality in which his care must be rooted is always the Christian mystery.

This explicit and implicit awareness of Christ's personal presence in a priest's ministry comes only through a disciplined separation from the busy world and a life of more intense recol-

9. Adrian van Kaam, *On Being Involved* (Denville, NJ: Dimension Books, 1970), pp. 69-101.

lected dwelling with the Lord. This separation is a difficult pill for most modern people to swallow. There is a tendency in all of us to want to live with a transfigured model of Christ rather than with the humble and foolish Christ. A young seminarian can easily become carried away by willfully projecting the ideal of a perfect world here and now, forgetting that Christ himself was humble enough to live the way of kenosis, or self-emptying. In the eyes of the world, a Lord who comes as a lamb is foolish and even mad, for he cuts across the grain of how we so often think the world should work and operate.

THE WAY OF KENOSIS:
THE "NAZARETH" EXPERIENCE

How do I live this kind of kenotic life in the seminary? The evangelist continues his Gospel with a very important insight when he writes:

> The next day, after Jesus had decided to leave for Galilee, he met Philip and said, "Follow me." . . . Philip found Nathanael and said to him, "We have found the one Moses wrote about in the Law, the one about whom the prophets wrote: he is Jesus son of Joseph, from Nazareth." "From Nazareth?" said Nathanael. "Can anything good come from that place?" "Come and see," replied Philip.
>
> (John 1:43-46)

When Nathanael stuck up his nose at the place called Nazareth, he was being very like ourselves. Would it not be better if we could say to our seminarians that Jesus came from a biblical Boston or New York? Coming from Nazareth is like saying Jesus comes from the least significant little town in one of our big metropolitan dioceses. In my own diocese, which is Boston, it would be like saying that Jesus came from Pepperell, a little town north of Boston whose recent claim to fame is that Henry Robinson, in his novel *The Cardinal,* made it the farthest out-post for assigning a priest to oblivion.

Every diocese has its little "Nazareth" where nothing too im-portant or relevant ever happens. For a world that is always waiting for a spectacular coming of the Messiah, it is just too difficult to believe that the Messiah, the lamb of God, came from a nowhere town.

This passage about Jesus' coming from Nazareth simply continues the tone of Christ's entire life. Jesus spent thirty years in an ordinary place preparing himself by growing in wisdom and understanding. Such is the milieu of a spiritually centered seminary. It is a very unspectacular and ordinary place to which a candidate for priesthood is called to come and see where Christ lives in the ordinary rhythms of life. It is a hidden place just as Christ's life in Nazareth was hidden. When Philip tells Nathanael that the one Moses and the prophets wrote about is just a carpenter's son, the poverty of this whole call to follow Christ is thrown into further relief. We keep coming back to the same motif. To follow Christ, to come and see where he lives, is not attractive in any human way to my pride. But such is the beauty of Christ. If he had come as a great scholar, a learned theologian, or a powerful king, I would be so blinded by those qualities that I might not see beyond these "little beyonds" to the "Big Beyond" of his divinity.

Christ knew better than I do that I am constantly rooted and enmeshed in a powerful pride system. If I cannot become great in my own right, I tend to want to link myself with a great person. I can become enthusiastic about a political figure, a sports hero, a poor man who has struck it rich. Witness today the popularity of state lotteries that promise instant wealth and fame. Listen to the advertising with which we are constantly bombarded. The world in which I live is attempting in countless ways to lock into my pride system and manipulate it.

Christ, on the other hand, comes to defuse this explosive and self-destructive energy. He comes as the helpless lamb, the totally vulnerable one. If he had come with the appearances of greatness, he would have fed right into my pride system. I would have liked him for the wrong reason. Even the Apostles succumbed to this temptation. They had a dispute over who was eventually going to sit at Christ's right and left hand, judging the twelve tribes of Israel. "'Can you drink the cup that I am going to drink?' They replied, 'We can.' 'Very well,' he said, 'you shall drink my cup, but as for seats at my right hand and my left, these are not mine to give'" (Matt. 20:22-23). The Apostles finally found out that following Christ was not much fun, for they all, save John, died in unpleasant ways. The cup that the lamb of God offers is completely foolish from the viewpoint of the relevant standards of the Western world.

Russian orthodox spirituality has preserved this tradition of the "fool of Christ," but the Western Church has too often become caught up in the transfigured image of the powerful Christ. Poverty is so irrelevant to our Western standards that we are constantly trying to "wash" our world into a sterile and pure perfection. We forget or never learned that a magnificent untapped richness can be present in material as well as in spiritual poverty. Mother Theresa of Calcutta, for example, is saying something important in her healing care for the kenotic Christ. She is never going to change or transfigure the slums, but she can live there and understand the mystery of Christ's presence in extreme poverty.[10]

The question "Can you drink the cup I am going to drink?" is the same question that each seminarian is asked when he accepts the invitation to come and follow Christ. Staying with Christ means choosing to enter a life whose whole orientation is to break down the rock of pride in order to build a new life on the true rock of Christ. The seminary is also a "poor city" like Nazareth. Priests are ordained from a seminary, and for the most part they do not like to return. Many active and busy priests look back on the seminary as a totally irrelevant place, a bad dream they tolerated in order to be ordained. Yet the semi-

10. Malcolm Muggeridge, *Something Beautiful For God: Mother Theresa of Calcutta* (New York, NY: Harper & Row, 1971).

nary is an important place of preparation, for it marks the beginning of a whole new journey into a life of spiritual poverty. Not to appreciate the seminary's important role, to want to escape this phase of spiritual purification and growth, is to want to live too much in the "busy city" of Jerusalem where all kinds of "relevant" events are happening. The seminarian who is allowed to be constantly away from the Nazareth experience of the seminary and too comfortably enmeshed in the Jerusalem experience of the world may eventually become the living contradiction of Christ's words: "I passed your word on to them, and the world hated them because they belong to the world no more than I belong to the world. . . . I am not asking you to remove them from the world but to protect them from the evil one. . . . Consecrate them in the truth" (John 17:14-17). The world may love the seminarian too much. He may also enjoy the world too much. He may forget that he is to live in the world but not be a part of it. He is consecrated in the truth of becoming the world's man of prayer and spiritual vision only by being able to draw apart and reflect deeply on the real meaning of his unique call in the Spirit. The seminary should provide this privileged space and time for spiritual preparation and formation.

To confuse the priorities of the Nazareth and Jerusalem experiences is to forget that Jesus did not begin his public life in Jerusalem. His whole life, beginning in Nazareth, the desert, and all the small towns of his early ministry, was a gradual journey toward Jerusalem. If the seminarian ignores this mystery, he will not have a deep enough rooting in the mystery of Christ's true meaning to point always to the Lord. He will not have spent enough time and attention ever really meeting the Lord in his place apart from the world, a place where he invites the true disciples to come and see.

THE SEMINARIAN IS SEEN BY CHRIST

When Jesus meets Nathanael he says: "'There is an Israelite

who deserves the name, incapable of deceit.' 'How do you know me?' said Nathanael. 'Before Philip came to call you,' said Jesus, 'I saw you under the fig tree.'" (John 1:47-49). Before a spiritual director meets the candidate for priesthood, it can be said that Jesus has already seen this young man in a special way. Philip continues the original pointing of John the Baptist. The candidate is always in a spiritual director's presence as one chosen by the Lord to follow, to come and see. Christ then said to Nathanael: "'You believe that just because I said: I saw you under the fig tree. You will see greater things than that.' And then he added, 'I tell you most solemnly, you will see heaven laid open and above the Son of Man, the angels of God ascending and descending'" (John 1:50-51). As spiritual director, I should live the solemn responsibility of laying open the heavenly presence by the witness of my life. Angels of God often are the messengers or messages of God. I am entrusted with letting the Lord reveal through my witness that this whole frightening and terrifying cosmos is really not frightening at all. In prayer, spiritual reading, meditation, liturgical celebration, counseling, and conferences, the heavens are laid open and the love and care of the Lord is coming down and going up. Heaven has already begun right here in the choice to come and see, to live with the lamb. In this new world, the Son of man has redeemed the world. It has lost its terror. I too can be a lamb if I accept that helplessness, vulnerability, loneliness, and bewilderment have been also redeemed. I no longer have to hide in my pride system. I can let go and relax. I can be open to the Lord in a new world that is now open to the transcendent mystery.

HUMBLY BEING MY REAL AND ORIGINAL SELF

One of the most important qualities of a good spiritual director is the virtue of humility. "Humility" and "human" come from the same Latin root, which is *humus. Humus* means "rooted in the earth."[11] A humble witness is one who recognizes who he really is and does not get caught up in an ideal self-presence. He recognizes his limitations and can comfortably work within such a framework. John the Baptist is again a striking example of such a man. John had been preaching and teaching his disciples with great success and acclaim. After awhile, Christ emerged more visibly, and some of John's disciples asked him this question:

> "Rabbi, the man who was with you on the far
> side of the Jordan, the man to whom you bore
> witness, is baptizing now, and everyone is going
> to him." John replied:
> "A man can lay claim only to what is given
> him from heaven.
> You yourselves can bear me out: I said, I myself
> am not the Christ; I am the one who has been sent
> in front of him.
> The bride is only for the bridegroom;
> and yet the bridegroom's friend,
> who stands there and listens,
> is glad when he hears the bridegroom's voice.
> This same joy I feel, and it is complete.
> He must grow greater,
> I must grow smaller. . . .
> He who comes from above
> is above all others;
> He who is born of the earth
> is earthly himself and speaks in an earthly way. . . ."
> (John 3:25-31)

MY ONLY CLAIM IS TO WHAT IS GIVEN FROM HEAVEN

John's declaration is a beautiful illustration of what we call discovering our spiritual identity. Each one of us has an eternal call from God. Each of us has a certain thing to do in life. Nobody knows exactly what he or she has to do. Everyone uncovers this original call during a lifetime. The important thing is to try

---

11. *Webster's New International Dictionary* (Springfield, MA: G. & C. Merriam Co., 1955), p. 1,212.

to be satisfied with what we have to do. John the Baptist was a precursor of the Lord. In the beginning, he was successful. Countless people came to him to be baptized. People identified with him very closely. It was a blow to his followers when another man, Jesus, began to baptize and preach. Jesus was now becoming more successful. John's disciples quite naturally began to complain. John's answer was a living sign of complete humility, of complete recognition of who he was called to be and nothing more: "A man can lay claim only to what is given him from heaven. . . ." (John 3:27). As a spiritual director of seminarians, I cannot claim anything. I cannot claim any success either in my private or my public life. All that I have has been given to me by the Lord. Anything that I share with seminarians is, ultimately, not mine. I can lay claim only to what has been given to me from heaven.

However, the disciples of John tried to claim that he had a kind of right to success. Because of his mortified ascetical life and his original charisma, they believed that people should come to him and him alone. The life of a good spiritual director can be similar. Candidates will have a tendency to cling to and feel safe with an understanding director. Yet a wise director must realize that anything he gives is not his own. He is present in seminary formation to point his directee toward the Lord. More and more he detaches the seminarian from his own presence as director and urges him to walk toward the Lord. The important thing is that the Lord turns to the disciple and says, "Come follow me." Christ can do so only if the directee has turned away from a cozy and secure "immanence"[12] with his director and is openly turned toward the Lord.

Another situation that John's humility helps a spiritual director understand is Christ's revealing himself in somebody else.

12. See Chapter 3, in which I discuss Adrian van Kaam's consideration of immanence as man's tendency to remain safe and secure. Transcendence is man's openness to new growth, new emergence.

Christ may make use of someone else on the seminary staff to reveal himself more intimately. The entire faculty community should be a fraternity of brothers in the Lord. Such a community has many unique and original talents and gifts to share with one another and with seminarians. At different times, however, I might begin to feel that "my private little specialty" of spiritual direction is being usurped. I begin to feel less good, less effective, less successful, and less needed. I may become resentful, envious, or jealous of another faculty member. But the interesting and humbling point is that Christ is always free to use whomever he likes. Christ may even use people who, in some way, may be less qualified than I. For example, he may choose a "foolish one to confound the wise" by making someone who is limited in some way the rector of the seminary or the head of the spiritual formation team. This person might not appreciate my "grand design" for spiritual renewal. However, Christ lets this person become my superior. Christ allows this to be. It is Christ appearing in this person no matter how imperfect this person may be. Others might sense the limitations of such a person, and I may begin to hear rumblings that students believe I would have been much more qualified to be in this position of leadership or authority. Some might feel strongly that it is not fair that such a "saintly" person as myself should have been bypassed or ignored. However, I must learn to say in my own heart what John was able to say so graciously: "A man can lay claim only to what is given him from heaven. . . ." (John 3:27). Maybe Christ gave me life, applause, and a privileged but temporary position. My time may be over. There will always be people who enter my life, who will come after me but rank before me. If my sense of identity depends on constant comparison with others, I will be eaten alive by resentment.[13] All that I can do in the hour that Christ

---

13. See Chapter 2. Here I discuss Max Scheler's consideration of resentment. Refer also to the appendices of *Personal Care and Pastoral Presence,* pp. 630-40, in which I include Henri Nouwen's discussion of resentment in seminary life.

calls me is what is important. Ultimately, the ministry is really Christ's.

The older I get, the more I may face the predicament of John. I will begin to see others going out to younger people. Other priest directors may come to take my place. If I can lay claim to only what is given me from heaven, then this natural rhythm of human life can be a graceful letting go. It will be okay to let others come and have their hour. I do not need to be angry; rather I can feel grateful that the privileged moments I have enjoyed with seminarians, or with anyone for that matter, are really gifts shared with me by the Lord. They are not mine. In the ministry of spiritual direction, this humble realization of who I am and who Christ really is becomes the foundation for becoming a grateful person.

TO BE SENT IN FRONT OF THE LORD

The profound lesson of John's Gospel is his repeated emphasis on this cardinal point that John the Baptist was only a witness. He was sent to speak for the light. He was not the light. As a spiritual director, I too have come to speak for the light. I am not the light. My whole life is a speaking for the light and not for myself. In this beautiful section of John's Gospel, John the Baptist comes back to his disciples and says: "You yourselves can bear me out: I said, I myself am not the Christ; I am the one who has been sent in front of him" (John 3:28). This statement can be truly said about all spiritual directors. As a spiritual director, I am sent in front of the Lord. It is a tremendous privilege to speak for the light by being sent in front of him. This awareness that I am sent in front of the Lord may diminish my self-centered preoccupation, worry, and anxiety. In a profound sense, I am a "front" man for the Lord in my association with seminarians.

A FRIEND OF THE BRIDEGROOM

Even in the seminary just as it was along the Jordan: "The bride is only for the bridegroom; and yet the bridegroom's friend, who stands there and listens, is glad when he hears the bridegroom's voice. This same joy I feel, and now it is complete" (John 3:29). The students and the spiritual director are only for the bridegroom who is Christ. As spiritual director, I am the friend of the bridegroom. I am one who stands there and listens. Being there and openly listening are the essence of what it means to be a caring *dasein*. [14] I am called to be there with the Lord as his friend. I am glad when I hear the bridegroom's voice and not my own. In this privileged way of care, I can feel a deep sense of joy and know that my work is complete when it is the Lord's voice that is heard and accepted. My little ego is not bruised because my Friend has been successful and I am here, just listening. His delight is my delight because we are companions and not competitors on the same Emmaus road.

HE MUST GROW GREATER; I MUST GROW SMALLER

John concludes his hymn of joy with the final commentary: "He must grow greater; I must grow smaller. He who comes from above is above all others; He who is born of the earth is earthly himself and speaks in an earthly way. . . ." (John 3:30-31). There is a tremendous joy in John the Baptist's humility. Christ must grow greater and John must grow smaller. In a few words, John summarizes the whole Christian mystery. As a spiritual director, I, too, must grow smaller and Christ must grow greater. It is not important whether I am learned, likeable, or successful. The only thing that is important is that Christ grows greater not only in my own life but in the lives of the seminarians entrusted to me for spiritual direction. I am born of

---

14. Refer to *Personal Care and Pastoral Presence,* pp. 22-24, wherein I discuss Martin Heidegger's consideration of man as defined by the German word *dasein,* which means "being-there."

the earth, and I can speak only in an earthly way. All my speaking, insofar as it is not transformed by Christ, is and remains an earthly speaking. Therefore, I can do little for those in my care. Insofar as Christ is speaking, insofar as he, who is above all others, touches in and through me the hearts and souls of seminarians, I can feel joy. To let that miracle of new life emerge, to let Christ emerge in the unique and original lives of seminarians, I must grow smaller and Christ must always grow greater. To accept Christ's invitation to come and see, to follow in his footsteps as a friend who is called to be in front of his presence in the lives of seminarians, is to speak for a light that the darkness of the world can never overpower.

AFFIRMATION BOOKS is an important part of the House of Affirmation, International Therapeutic Center for Clergy and Religious, founded by Sr. Anna Polcino, S.C.M.M., M.D.

3 5282 00004 8184